W9-BGF-919

Oregon Focus On

Fractions & Decimals

SM curriculum

Stage 1

AUTHORS

Shannon McCaw

Beth Armstrong • Matt McCaw • Sarah Schuhl • Michelle Terry • Scott Valway

COVER PHOTOGRAPH

Vista House
Built in 1916, the Vista House perches atop a cliff in the
Columbia River Gorge. Along with the majestic views,
the Vista House has a museum and interpretive center
for visitors to enjoy.
©iStockphoto.com/Jeanne Hatch

ISBN: 978-1-935033-00-4

ABOUT THE AUTHORS

SERIES AUTHOR

Shannon McCaw is a classroom teacher and consultant. She has taught mathematics in the Newberg and Parkrose School Districts. She has been trained in Professional Learning Communities, Differentiated Instruction and Critical Friends. Shannon currently works with math teachers from over 40 districts around the State of Oregon. Her expertise lies in Oregon standards, curriculum alignment and assessment practices.

CONTRIBUTING AUTHORS

Beth Armstrong has been an elementary school teacher in the Beaverton School District. She has received training in Talented and Gifted Instruction. She is currently completing her Masters in Curriculum and Instruction from Washington State University.

Matt McCaw has been a classroom teacher and special education case-manager in the Newberg, Centennial and Parkrose School Districts in Oregon. Matt has been trained in Differentiated Instruction, Professional Learning Communities, Critical Friends Groups and Understanding Poverty. He currently teaches math at Parkrose High School.

Sarah Schuhl has been a classroom teacher in Union, Lake Oswego and Centennial School Districts in Oregon. She has been trained in Assessment for Learning, Professional Learning Communities, Advanced Placement and Instructional Coaching. She currently serves as the Math Instructional Coach at Centennial High School.

Michelle Terry has been a classroom teacher in the Estacada and Newberg School Districts in Oregon. Michelle has received training in Professional Learning Communities, Critical Friends, and ELL Instructional Strategies. She currently fills the role of a Teacher on Special Assignment with a focus on math curriculum and instruction at Newberg High School.

Scott Valway has been a classroom teacher in the Tigard-Tualatin, Newberg and Parkrose School Districts in Oregon. Scott has been trained in Differentiated Instruction, Professional Learning Communities, Critical Friends, Discovering Algebra, and Pre-Advanced Placement. He currently teaches math at Parkrose High School.

OREGON CORE STANDARDS

The complete set of Oregon Core Standards can be found at www.ode.state.or.us/go/math. This book focuses on the highlighted core standards shown below.

GRADE 6

It is essential that these standards be addressed in contexts that promote problem solving, reasoning, communication, making connections, and designing and analyzing representations.

6.1	<u>Number and Operations:</u> **Develop an understanding of and fluency with multiplication and division of fractions and decimals.**
6.1.1	Select and use appropriate strategies to estimate fraction and decimal products and quotients.
6.1.2	Use and analyze a variety of strategies, including models, for solving problems with multiplication and division of fractions.
6.1.3	Use and analyze a variety of strategies, including models, for solving problems with multiplication and division of decimals.
6.1.4	Develop fluency with efficient procedures for multiplying and dividing fractions and decimals and justify why the procedures work.
6.1.5	Apply the inverse relationship between multiplication and division to make sense of procedures for multiplying and dividing fractions and justify why they work.
6.1.6	Apply the properties of operations to simplify calculations.
6.1.7	Use the relationship between common decimals and fractions to solve problems including problems involving measurement.

6.2	<u>Number and Operations and Probability:</u> **Connect ratio, rate, and percent to multiplication and division.**
6.2.1	Develop, analyze, and apply the meaning of ratio, rate, and percent to solve problems.
6.2.2	Determine decimal and percent equivalents for common fractions, including approximations.
6.2.3	Understand the meaning of probability and represent probabilities as ratios, decimals, and percents.
6.2.4	Determine simple probabilities, both experimental and theoretical.
6.2.5	Develop the concept of π as the ratio of the circumference of a circle to its diameter.

6.3	<u>Algebra:</u> **Write, interpret, and use mathematical expressions and equations.**
6.3.1	Use order of operations to simplify expressions that may include exponents and grouping symbols.
6.3.2	Develop the meanings and uses of variables.
6.3.3	Write, evaluate, and use expressions and formulas to solve problems.
6.3.4	Identify and represent equivalent expressions (e.g., different ways to see a pattern).
6.3.5	Represent, analyze, and determine relationships and patterns using tables, graphs, words and when possible, symbols.
6.3.6	Recognize that the solutions of an equation are the values of the variables that make the equation true.
6.3.7	Solve one-step equations by using number sense, properties of operations, and the idea of maintaining equality on both sides of an equation.

Reprinted with permission from the Oregon Department of Education. All rights reserved.

OREGON FOCUS ON FRACTIONS AND DECIMALS
CONTENTS IN BRIEF

BLOCK 1 ~ UNDERSTANDING FRACTIONS

BLOCK 2 ~ ADDING AND SUBTRACTING FRACTIONS

BLOCK 3 ~ MULTIPLYING AND DIVIDING FRACTIONS

BLOCK 4 ~ DECIMALS

HOW TO USE YOUR MATH BOOK

Your math book has features that will help you be successful in this course. Use this guide to help you understand how to use this book.

LESSON TARGET

 Look in this box at the beginning of every lesson to know what you will be learning about in each lesson.

VOCABULARY

Each new vocabulary word is printed in red. The definition can be found with the word. You can also find the definition of the word in the glossary which is in the back of this book.

EXPLORE!

Some lessons have **EXPLORE!** activities which allow you to discover mathematical concepts. Look for these activities in the Table of Contents and in lessons next to the purple line.

EXAMPLES

Examples are useful because they remind you how to work through different types of problems. Look for the word **EXAMPLE** and the green line.

HELPFUL HINTS

Helpful hints and important things to remember can be found in green callout boxes.

BLUE BOXES

A blue box holds important information or a process that will be used in that lesson. Not every lesson has a blue box.

 This calculator icon will appear in Lessons and Exercises where a calculator is needed. Your teacher may want you to use your calculator at other times, too. If you are unsure, make sure to ask if it is the right time to use it.

EXERCISES

The **EXERCISES** are a place for you to find practice problems to determine if you understand the lesson's target. You can find selected answers in the back of this book so you can check your progress.

REVIEW

The **REVIEW** provides a set of problems for you to practice concepts you have already learned in this book. The **REVIEW** follows the **EXERCISES** in each lesson. There is also a **REVIEW** section at the end of each Block.

TIC-TAC-TOE ACTIVITIES

Each Block has a Tic-Tac-Toe board at the beginning with activities that extend beyond the Oregon Core Standards. The Tic-Tac-Toe activities described on the board can be found throughout each Block in yellow boxes.

CAREER FOCUS

At the end of each Block, you will find an autobiography of an Oregon resident. Each person explains what they like about their job and how math is used in their career.

OREGON FOCUS ON MATH
STAGE 1

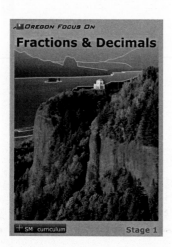

LETTER FROM THE AUTHORS

Dear Student,

This textbook was specifically designed for you. As a student learning math in Oregon, you are responsible for learning three areas of mathematics each year. Each year you will take a state assessment that tests your skills in these areas.

Stage 1	*Focus on Fractions and Decimals*
	Focus on Ratios, Rates and Percents
	Focus on Introductory Algebra
Stage 2	*Focus on Rational Numbers and Equations*
	Focus on Proportionality
	Focus on Surface Area and Volume
Stage 3	*Focus on Linear Equations*
	Focus on Data Analysis
	Focus on Lines and Angles

When you successfully finish these areas, you will be ready to enter Algebra I. For the graduating class of 2014 and beyond, you will need 3 credits of mathematics in high school that are at the Algebra I level and above.

It is important that you give your best effort in math class as everyone can be good at math if they try. If you have questions, ask your teacher, a friend or a parent. Do not be shy; nearly everyone struggles with math sometimes.

In these books you will find information about places and events from all across the state of Oregon. We hope you enjoy learning about your state. You may even find something about the city or town you live in!

Sincerely,

Shannon McCaw

Matt McCaw

Beth Armstrong

Sarah Schuhl

Scott Valway

Michelle Terry

BLOCK 1 ~ FRACTIONS AND DECIMALS
UNDERSTANDING FRACTIONS

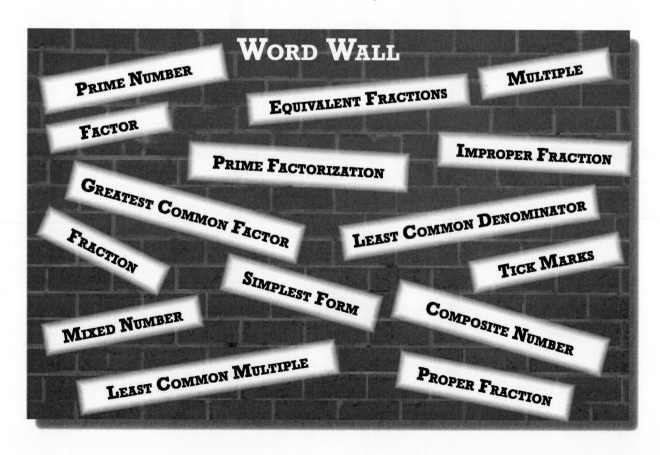

WORD WALL

PRIME NUMBER   EQUIVALENT FRACTIONS   MULTIPLE

FACTOR

PRIME FACTORIZATION   IMPROPER FRACTION

GREATEST COMMON FACTOR   LEAST COMMON DENOMINATOR

FRACTION

SIMPLEST FORM   TICK MARKS

MIXED NUMBER   COMPOSITE NUMBER

LEAST COMMON MULTIPLE   PROPER FRACTION

BLOCK 1 ~ UNDERSTANDING FRACTIONS
TIC - TAC - TOE

EXPLORE PRIME

Investigate prime numbers. Decide if there is a pattern for finding prime numbers.

See page 7 for details.

CONCAVE AND CONVEX

Create concave and convex figures using seven different line segments.

See page 38 for details.

FAVORITES

Survey at least 50 people. Write results as fractions. Create a graph to display your results.

See page 25 for details.

OCCUPATIONS

Research and write about an occupation that uses fractions on a daily basis.

See page 7 for details.

EDIBLE FRACTIONS

Use a bag of multicolored candies to write, simplify and order fractions.

See page 20 for details.

FRACTION GAME

Make a game using equivalent fractions.

See page 12 for details.

EQUIVALENT FRACTIONS

Make a poster to display sets of equivalent fractions.

See page 12 for details.

COINS AND FRACTIONS

Create a table that displays the worth of coins as fractions of a dollar.

See page 34 for details.

RECIPE MIX-UP

Create a Recipe Mix-Up cookbook using improper and equivalent fractions.

See page 29 for details.

GREATEST COMMON FACTOR

Find the greatest common factor (GFC) of a set of numbers.

Factors are whole numbers that can be multiplied together to find a product. For example, 2 and 4 are factors of 8 because $2 \times 4 = 8$.

When a whole number has only two possible factors (1 and the number itself), it is called a prime number. A whole number larger than one is called a composite number when it has more than two factors.

EXAMPLE 1

Determine if 12 is a prime or composite number.

SOLUTION

List the pairs of numbers that have a product of 12. These are the factors of 12.

1×12	12×1
2×6	6×2
3×4	4×3

These are the same factors in reverse order.

List each factor once, even if it is repeated.

The factors of 12 are 1, 2, 3, 4, 6 and 12.

There are more than two factors so the number 12 is composite.

The greatest common factor (GCF) of two or more numbers is the greatest factor that is common to all the numbers. The greatest common factor can be used to solve problems involving real-life situations.

EXPLORE!   **UNIVERSITY SALES**

Bracken had 36 University of Oregon shirts and 42 Oregon State University shirts to sell. He wants to stack them in piles that would all have the same number of shirts. He does not want to mix the two types of shirts. What is the greatest number of shirts that can be stacked in each pile? Find the GCF of 36 and 42.

Step 1: Find all factors of 36 by filling the boxes with the missing factors. Make a list of all factors of 36.

$\square \times 36$ $2 \times \square$ $\square \times 12$ $4 \times \square$ $\square \times 6$

Step 2: Find all factors of 42 by filling the boxes with the missing factors. Make a list of all factors of 42.

$1 \times \square$ $2 \times \square$ $3 \times \square$ $\square \times 7$

Step 3: Circle the common factors. Common factors are factors that are the same for both 36 and 42.

Step 4: Draw a Venn diagram like the one to the right on a sheet of paper. Write "Factors of 36" on the outside of the left circle and "Factors of 42" on the outside of the right circle.

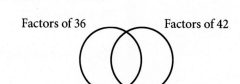

Factors of 36   Factors of 42

Step 5: Place all factors on the Venn diagram. The factors that both numbers have in common go in the overlapping part of the circles.
The remaining factors of 36 go in the left circle.
The remaining factors of 42 go in the right circle.

Factors of 36   Factors of 42

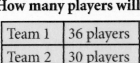

Step 6: Look at the common factors where the circles overlap. Circle the largest number. This is the greatest common factor (GCF).

Step 7: Use the GCF to answer the question in the problem at the beginning of the Explore! in a complete sentence.

Step 8: Repeat **Steps 1-6** to find the GCF of the following pairs of numbers:
   a. 15 and 25   **b.** 18 and 30   **c.** 24 and 40

There are other methods to find the greatest common factor. Prime factorization is shown when any composite number is written as a product of all its prime factors.

EXAMPLE 2   **Two local teams went to soccer camp together. At the camp the teams were asked to split into equal amounts for cabin groups. The players did not want to room with players from other teams. The camp directors want the largest number possible in each cabin. How many players will be in each cabin?**

Team 1	36 players
Team 2	30 players

SOLUTION   Use prime factors to find the GCF. Prime factors are factors that are prime numbers.

Write each number as products of two factors.

Continue to write each number as products of two factors until only factors that are prime numbers remain.

$$36$$
$$4 \times 9$$
$$2 \times 2 \quad 3 \times 3$$

$$30$$
$$6 \times 5$$
$$2 \times 3 \quad 5$$

Write the factors out for each number. This is called the prime factorization. Highlight the common prime factors.

$$36 = 2 \times 2 \times 3 \times 3 \quad 30 = 2 \times 3 \times 5$$

Find the product of the common prime factors. This is the GCF.

GCF = $2 \times 3 = 6$. The GCF is 6.

Six players will be in each cabin.

EXAMPLE 3

Reagan Middle School students were asked to sit in equal rows for the assembly. There were 98 sixth graders, 84 seventh graders and 112 eighth graders. The teachers did not want grade levels sitting together, but the rows were to be as wide as possible. How many students should sit in each row?

SOLUTION

List the factors of each number. Highlight the common factors.

Factors of 98: 1, 2, 7, 14, 49, 98
Factors of 84: 1, 2, 3, 4, 6, 7, 12, 14, 21, 28, 42, 84
Factors of 112: 1, 2, 4, 7, 8, 14, 16, 28, 56, 112

Find the GCF.

The GCF of 98, 84 and 112 is 14.

Fourteen students should sit in each row.

FIND THE GREATEST COMMON FACTOR

1. List the factors for each number.
2. Highlight the common factors.
3. Identify the GCF (greatest common factor).

EXERCISES

List the factors of each number. State whether each number is prime or composite.

1. 4 **2.** 3 **3.** 8

4. 7 **5.** 14 **6.** 20

7. 29 **8.** 16 **9.** 27

10. Alexis had 8 bracelets and 10 necklaces. She wanted to put equal amounts of each item into small travel containers. She did not want to mix the bracelets and necklaces. What is the largest number of items she could put in a travel container?

   a. Draw a Venn diagram. Put the number "8" on one side and "10" on the other side.

8   10

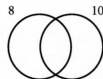

   b. List all factors for both numbers. Highlight the common factors.
   c. Place all uncommon factors for the 1st number in the left circle.
   d. Place all uncommon factors for the 2nd number in the right circle.
   e. Place the factors both numbers have in common in the overlapping part of the circles.
   f. What is the GCF?

Copy the following Venn diagrams. Write the factors on the Venn diagrams. Find the greatest common factor for each set of numbers.

11. 9   12

GCF =

12. 15   20

GCF =

13. 54   64

GCF =

List the factors for each number. Circle the greatest common factor for each set.

14. 6:
3:

15. 9:
6:

16. 12:
18:

17. 48:
32:
64:

18. 45:
60:
30:

19. 24:
40:
54:

Use prime factorization to find the greatest common factor of each set of numbers.

20. Tyler had 45 baseball cards and 54 basketball cards. He organized them into equal rows for a display. He did not want to mix the basketball and baseball cards in a row. What was the greatest number of cards in each row?

    a. Write each number as the product of any two of its factors.
    b. Continue to write each factor as the product of two factors until only prime factors remain.
    c. Write the prime factorization for each original number. Highlight the common prime factors.
    d. Find the product of the common prime factors.
    e. What is the GCF?

21. 18 and 24

22. 64 and 80

23. 84 and 56

24. Two sixth grade classes went to the local theater to watch a movie. They reserved seats ahead of time so each class could sit together in equal rows. One class had 28 students and the other had 21 students. What is the greatest number of students that could sit in each row?

25. Camilla separated prizes for games at the carnival. She had 72 Choco Bars and 90 Peanut Blitzes. She put the most candy bars possible in each bag without mixing the two types. Each bag needed an equal amount of candy. How many candy bars did she put in each bag?

26. This lesson contained three methods to find the greatest common factor: Venn diagrams, lists and prime factorization. Which method do you like best? Why?

Tic-Tac-Toe ~ Explore Prime

A prime number is a whole number larger than 1 that is the product of only two factors, 1 and itself. All other numbers are called composite numbers.

1. Copy the chart. Fill in the numbers from 2 through 50. Explain how you found the prime numbers. Give examples of at least 3 factors for each composite number.

Prime	Composite
$2 = 2 \times 1$	$4 = 4 \times 1$ or 2×2
$3 = 3 \times 1$	$6 = 6 \times 1$ or 2×3

2. Is there a pattern for finding prime numbers? Research prime numbers on the internet or in books. Write on one researcher's ideas about patterns with prime numbers. Include where you found the information (the exact web-site, book, etc.) in your paper.

Tic-Tac-Toe ~ Occupations

Many people use fractions in their daily work. Look at different occupations where people use fractions in their jobs. Pick one occupation to research.

Here are some things to look for.
- **a.** What do people in that occupation do daily?
- **b.** Why is that occupation necessary in our world?
- **c.** How do people in that occupation use fractions?

Create a magazine spread (1-2 pages) with your research.

1. Write an article that includes the important information from your research. Be sure to include answers to the three questions above.

2. Choose to take, print or draw one or more pictures for the spread.

Possible article ideas:
- Write the article as an interview between you (the magazine publisher) and a person in that occupation.
- Write the article as your view of "a day in the life of a person who works in..."
- Create a fictional person who is in that occupation. Write the article from his/her viewpoint.
- Write letters from fictional people in that occupation to your magazine explaining different aspects of their job.

EQUIVALENT FRACTIONS

Write equivalent fractions.

A recent survey asked girls and boys how they spend their free time. Three out of six girls said they spend their free time playing sports. One-half of the boys said they spend their free time playing sports. The results of the survey can be written using fractions.

A fraction is a number written as $\dfrac{\text{numerator}}{\text{denominator}}$.

A fraction represents part of a whole number. The denominator of a fraction cannot be 0. The line between the numerator and denominator can be read "out of". In the survey above, $\frac{3}{6}$ of the girls and $\frac{1}{2}$ of the boys said they spend their free time playing sports.

There are times when information needs to be compared to make it easier to understand. Equivalent fractions allow you to determine whether two fractions are equal. Equivalent fractions are two fractions that name the same amount.

To compare the fraction of girls that play sports to the fraction of boys that play sports, you can use models.

Draw two equal-sized rectangles. Each rectangle represents one whole unit.

Divide each rectangle into equal-sized sections using the denominator to determine the number of sections.

$\frac{3}{6}$

$\frac{1}{2}$

Use the value of the numerator to determine the number of sections to color in for each rectangle.

$\frac{3}{6}$

$\frac{1}{2}$

The same amount of each rectangle is colored. This means that $\frac{3}{6}$ is equivalent to $\frac{1}{2}$. According to the survey, the same portion of girls play sports in their free time as boys.

EXAMPLE 1

Use multiplication to find the missing number in the equivalent fractions.

a. $\dfrac{1}{2} = \dfrac{\square}{8}$

b. $\dfrac{3}{8} = \dfrac{6}{\square}$

SOLUTIONS

a. Make the denominators equivalent by multiplying 2 by 4.

$$\dfrac{1}{2} \overset{\times 4}{=} \dfrac{\square}{8}$$

Since the denominator was multiplied by 4, the numerator must also be multiplied by 4.

$$\dfrac{1}{2} \overset{\times 4}{=} \dfrac{4}{8}$$

The missing number is 4.

b. Make the numerators equivalent by multiplying 3 by 2.

$$\dfrac{3}{8} \overset{\times 2}{=} \dfrac{6}{\square}$$

Since the numerator was multiplied by 2, you must multiply the denominator by 2.

$$\dfrac{3}{8} = \dfrac{6}{16} {\scriptstyle \times 2}$$

The missing number is 16.

EXPLORE! CREATING EQUIVALENT FRACTIONS

Step 1: Choose a fraction from the purple box. Create a model of this fraction using fraction tiles. Draw or trace the fraction on paper. Write the fraction below the drawing.

$$\dfrac{3}{6}$$

$\dfrac{4}{8}$	$\dfrac{3}{12}$	$\dfrac{6}{10}$	$\dfrac{2}{8}$	$\dfrac{6}{12}$	$\dfrac{9}{12}$
$\dfrac{4}{6}$	$\dfrac{2}{10}$	$\dfrac{4}{12}$	$\dfrac{2}{12}$	$\dfrac{10}{12}$	$\dfrac{3}{6}$
$\dfrac{5}{10}$	$\dfrac{2}{6}$	$\dfrac{4}{10}$	$\dfrac{6}{8}$	$\dfrac{8}{12}$	$\dfrac{8}{10}$

Step 2: Use the fraction tiles to make an equivalent fraction with a smaller denominator. Record this on your paper to show that the two fractions are equivalent.

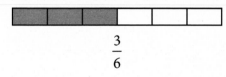

$$\dfrac{3}{6} = \dfrac{1}{2}$$

Step 3: Repeat **Steps 1-2** for four additional fractions from the purple box.

Step 4: Compare each of your fractions from the purple box to the equivalent fractions you formed. Were the original numerator and denominator multiplied or divided by a number to get the new fraction?

Step 5: Try to find equivalent fractions with smaller numerators and denominators for the fractions below without using a model.

$$\frac{10}{30} \qquad\qquad \frac{6}{12} \qquad\qquad \frac{15}{20}$$

EXAMPLE 2

Use division to find the missing number in the equivalent fractions.

a. $\dfrac{8}{16} = \dfrac{\square}{8}$ b. $\dfrac{12}{36} = \dfrac{1}{\square}$

SOLUTIONS

a. Make the denominators equivalent by dividing 16 by 2.

The denominator was divided by 2.
The numerator must also be divided by 2.

The missing number is 4.

$$\frac{8}{16} = \frac{\square}{8}$$
$$\overset{\div 2}{}$$

$$\overset{\div 2}{\frac{8}{16}} = \frac{4}{8}$$

b. Make the numerators equivalent by dividing 12 by 12.

The numerator was divided by 12.
The denominator must also be divided by 12.

The missing number is 3.

$$\overset{\div 12}{\frac{12}{36}} = \frac{1}{\square}$$

$$\frac{12}{36} = \frac{1}{3}\ _{\div 12}$$

EXERCISES

1. Use models to determine if $\frac{1}{3}$ is equivalent to $\frac{2}{6}$.

   a. Copy the two rectangles below.

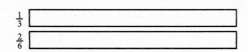

   b. Divide the first rectangle into 3 equal-sized sections.
      Divide the second rectangle into 6 equal-sized sections.
   c. Color in the number of sections given by the numerator of
      each fraction.
   d. Compare the two models. Are the fractions equivalent? Explain your answer.

Use models to show whether or not each pair of fractions is equivalent.

2. $\frac{1}{2}$ and $\frac{2}{4}$

3. $\frac{2}{5}$ and $\frac{3}{6}$

4. $\frac{1}{4}$ and $\frac{3}{8}$

5. Serj decided to use rectangular fraction tiles to show whether or not $\frac{5}{8}$ is equivalent to $\frac{3}{4}$. Look at Serj's model below. Are the fractions equivalent? How do you know?

6. Use rectangular tiles to show whether or not $\frac{4}{6}$ is equivalent to $\frac{2}{3}$.

Use multiplication to find the missing number for each equivalent fraction.

7. $\frac{1}{2} = \frac{\square}{8}$

8. $\frac{5}{6} = \frac{\square}{30}$

9. $\frac{3}{5} = \frac{18}{\square}$

10. $\frac{2}{3} = \frac{14}{\square}$

11. $\frac{1}{10} = \frac{\square}{30}$

12. $\frac{6}{7} = \frac{60}{\square}$

Use division to find the missing number for each equivalent fraction.

13. $\frac{10}{60} = \frac{1}{\square}$

14. $\frac{24}{64} = \frac{3}{\square}$

15. $\frac{8}{10} = \frac{\square}{5}$

16. $\frac{25}{35} = \frac{\square}{7}$

17. $\frac{12}{54} = \frac{2}{\square}$

18. $\frac{12}{14} = \frac{6}{\square}$

Write two fractions that are equivalent to each fraction.

19. $\frac{1}{3}$

20. $\frac{6}{12}$

21. $\frac{4}{10}$

22. $\frac{2}{8}$

23. $\frac{6}{9}$

24. $\frac{10}{25}$

25. Jedediah told his mom that $\frac{3}{9}$ of his chores were completed. His mother asked, "Are you telling me that $\frac{1}{3}$ of your chores are done?" How should he answer this question? Explain your reasoning.

26. Mykesha gave away 24 of the 30 sticks of gum in her pack.
   a. Write a fraction to represent the portion of gum she gave away.
   b. Write an equivalent fraction with a smaller numerator and denominator to represent the portion of gum she gave away.

REVIEW

List the factors of each number. State whether the number is prime or composite.

27. 11   **28.** 24   **29.** 39

Find the GCF of each pair of numbers using any method.

30. 10 and 30   **31.** 20 and 24   **32.** 42 and 72

TIC-TAC-TOE ~ FRACTION GAME

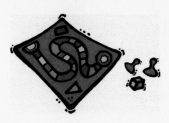

Step 1: Draw a game board on a piece of poster board with a starting place and more than sixteen squares that lead to an ending place.

Step 2: Write at least 8 different fractions in simplest form, one on each square, not including the starting point. You may use the same fraction up to two times.

Step 3: Write 3 equivalent fractions on small cards for each simplified fraction you wrote on your game board. (There will be at least 24 cards.)

Step 4: Write directions for your game. *Examples:* Do players go backward if they draw a card that has a fraction that is equivalent to one behind them but none in front of them? How do they get to the ending place? Are there places on the game board where they are stuck until they can answer a specific question with fractions?

Step 5: Try the game with your family or friends to make sure it works.

Step 6: Bring your game to class to play.

TIC-TAC-TOE ~ EQUIVALENT FRACTIONS

Common fractions are fractions used in our world. For example, they are fractions used in cooking, sewing, woodworking, etc. Some examples of common fractions are:

$$\frac{1}{2} \quad \frac{1}{4} \quad \frac{3}{4} \quad \frac{1}{3} \quad \frac{2}{3} \quad \frac{1}{8}$$

Write three equivalent fractions for each fraction above. Make a poster to display the sets of fractions. Use models to show each common fraction and its equivalent fractions.

SIMPLIFYING FRACTIONS

 Write fractions in simplest form.

A fraction is in **simplest form** when the numerator's and the denominator's only common factor is 1. Change a fraction into simplest form by repeatedly dividing by common factors until the only common factor between the numerator and denominator is 1.

EXPLORE!   **FRACTION HOMEWORK**

Five friends from different math classes worked on their fraction homework. The table shows the number of problems each student completed out of the total number assigned.

Name	Problems Completed	Problems Assigned
Marisol	12	20
Kevin	15	18
Oscar	30	40
Nancy	24	36
Julie	20	25

Step 1: Write a fraction to represent the portion of homework each student completed.

Step 2: Marisol wants to represent the portion of problems she has completed in simplest form. She needs to find a common factor of 12 and 20. What is one common factor of 12 and 20? Divide the numerator and denominator by this number to create an equivalent fraction.

Step 3: Look at the equivalent fraction you wrote in **Step 2**. Is there another common factor between the numerator and denominator of the fraction? If so, divide both parts of the fraction by this number to create another equivalent fraction. Continue doing this until the only common factor of the numerator and denominator is 1. This fraction is now in simplest form.

Step 4: Repeat this process for the other students. Write a fraction in simplest form to represent the portion of homework each student has completed.

EXAMPLE 1

SOLUTION

Use common factors to write $\frac{24}{30}$ in simplest form.

One common factor of 24 and 30 is 2.
Divide the numerator and denominator by 2.

$$\frac{24}{30} \overset{\div 2}{\underset{\div 2}{=}} \frac{12}{15}$$

A common factor of 12 and 15 is 3.
Divide the numerator and denominator by 3.

$$\frac{12}{15} \overset{\div 3}{\underset{\div 3}{=}} \frac{4}{5}$$

The only common factor between 4 and 5 is 1.
The fraction $\frac{4}{5}$ is in simplest form.

You can also use the greatest common factor to write a fraction in simplest form. Dividing the numerator and denominator by the greatest common factor will show the fraction in its simplest form.

WRITING FRACTIONS IN SIMPLEST FORM

Divide the numerator and denominator by common factors until the only common factor is 1.

OR

Divide the numerator and denominator by the greatest common factor (GCF).

EXAMPLE 2

SOLUTION

Use the greatest common factor to write $\frac{10}{40}$ in simplest form.

Find the factors of 10.   1, 2, 5, ⑩

Find the factors of 40.   1, 2, 4, 5, 8, ⑩ 20, 40

The GCF is 10.

Divide both the numerator and the denominator by 10.

$$\frac{10}{40} \overset{\div 10}{\underset{\div 10}{=}} \frac{1}{4}$$

The fraction $\frac{1}{4}$ is in simplest form.

EXAMPLE 3

Use the graph to determine the fraction of students who chose Track & Field as their favorite sport. Write the answer in simplest form.

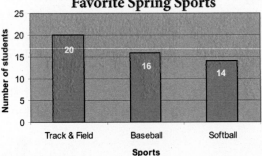

SOLUTION

Write the fraction by taking the number of students who chose Track & Field out of the total number of students.

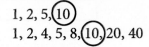

$$\frac{\text{number of students who chose Track \& Field}}{\text{total number of students}}$$

Find the total number of students surveyed.   20 + 16 + 14 = 50

Fifty students were surveyed. The denominator will be 50.

EXAMPLE 3
SOLUTION
(CONTINUED)

Twenty students said Track & Field was their favorite sport so 20 is the numerator.

$$\frac{20}{50}$$

Simplify the fraction. Use the common factor method or the GCF method.

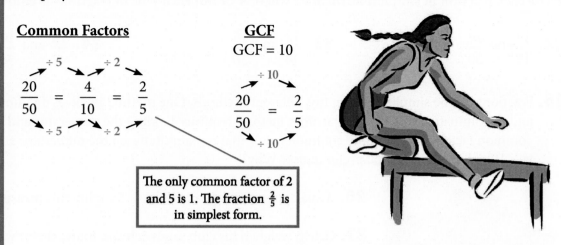

Common Factors

$$\frac{20}{50} = \frac{4}{10} = \frac{2}{5}$$

$\div 5 \quad \div 2$

$\div 5 \quad \div 2$

GCF

GCF = 10

$$\frac{20}{50} = \frac{2}{5}$$

$\div 10$

$\div 10$

The only common factor of 2 and 5 is 1. The fraction $\frac{2}{5}$ is in simplest form.

Two-fifths of the students said Track & Field is their favorite sport.

EXERCISES

Use common factors to write each fraction in simplest form. If the fraction is already in simplest form, write *simplest form*.

1. $\frac{9}{10}$
2. $\frac{15}{25}$
3. $\frac{16}{20}$

4. $\frac{48}{72}$
5. $\frac{32}{61}$
6. $\frac{30}{80}$

Use the GCF to write each fraction in simplest form. If it is already in simplest form, write *simplest form*.

7. $\frac{5}{15}$
8. $\frac{18}{30}$
9. $\frac{13}{18}$

10. $\frac{21}{28}$
11. $\frac{22}{77}$
12. $\frac{16}{28}$

Write each fraction in simplest form. Use any method.

13. $\frac{12}{20}$
14. $\frac{40}{60}$
15. $\frac{15}{45}$

16. $\frac{16}{24}$
17. $\frac{6}{16}$
18. $\frac{28}{42}$

19. $\frac{6}{15}$

20. $\frac{21}{84}$

21. $\frac{24}{27}$

Write each fraction in simplest form. State whether or not each pair of fractions is equivalent.

22. $\frac{10}{15}$ and $\frac{20}{30}$

23. $\frac{12}{24}$ and $\frac{16}{36}$

24. $\frac{14}{42}$ and $\frac{10}{36}$

25. Fractions can be simplified using two different methods. One method involves dividing the numerator and denominator by the GCF. The other method requires dividing the numerator and denominator by common factors until the only common factor that remains between the numerator and denominator is 1. Which method do you prefer to use? Why?

26. A snake measured $\frac{20}{25}$ meter long. Simplify this measurement.

27. Ochen weighed his club sandwich and found that it weighed $\frac{6}{16}$ pound. Simplify this measurement.

28. A student claims that $\frac{21}{41}$ is in simplest form. Do you agree? Explain.

Use the following graph. Write each fraction in simplest form.

29. What fraction of students chose to read *Charlie and the Chocolate Factory*?

30. What fraction of students chose to read *A Wrinkle in Time*?

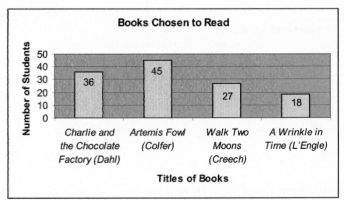

REVIEW

Write two fractions that are equivalent to each given fraction.

31. $\frac{1}{3}$

32. $\frac{9}{27}$

33. $\frac{40}{50}$

Use multiplication or division to find the missing number in each pair of equivalent fractions.

34. $\frac{1}{3} = \frac{4}{\square}$

35. $\frac{18}{27} = \frac{\square}{3}$

36. $\frac{22}{42} = \frac{11}{\square}$

LEAST COMMON MULTIPLE

 Find the least common multiple for a set of numbers.
Find the least common denominator for a set of fractions.

Dean and Kai volunteered together today at the recreation center. Dean volunteers every four days. Kai volunteers every five days. When will they be at the recreation center together again?

Dean's volunteer days ☐

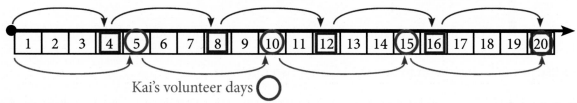

Look at the model above. The multiples of 4 are in blue squares and the multiples of 5 are circled in red. A **multiple** is the product of a given number and a whole number. The **least common multiple (LCM)** is the smallest multiple (not zero) that is common to two or more given numbers. By using the LCM, you can see that Dean and Kai will volunteer together in 20 days. That is the first time the ○ and ☐ are on the same number.

LEAST COMMON MULTIPLE (LCM)

List the multiples of the given numbers until you find the first multiple that is common to all given numbers.

OR

Use prime factorization of the given numbers to identify prime factors. Identify the common prime factors. Find the product of the common prime factors and any remaining factors.

EXAMPLE 1 | **List the first five non-zero multiples of 3 and 6. Find the LCM.**

SOLUTION | Write the multiples of 3 and 6.

$3 \times 1 = 3$ $6 \times 1 = 6$
$3 \times 2 = 6$ $6 \times 2 = 12$
$3 \times 3 = 9$ $6 \times 3 = 18$
$3 \times 4 = 12$ $6 \times 4 = 24$
$3 \times 5 = 15$ $6 \times 5 = 30$

Multiples of 3   Multiples of 6

> The first number to appear in both lists is 6.

List the multiples for each number.

Multiples of 3: 3, 6, 9, 12, 15…
Multiples of 6: 6, 12, 18, 24, 30…

The least common multiple (LCM) is 6.

EXAMPLE 2

Courtney and Kaysha are cousins. Courtney visits her grandparents every 30 days. Kaysha visits her grandparents every 20 days. They both visited their grandparents today. How long will it be before they are together at their grandparents' house on the same day?

SOLUTION

List the multiples of each number.

20: 20, 40, 60, 80, 100, 120, 140, 160, 180, ...

30: 30, 60, 90, 120, 150, 180, ...

Find the common multiples.

Common multiples of 20 and 30: 60, 120, 180

Identify the LCM. LCM = 60

Courtney and Kaysha will be at their grandparents' house together in 60 days.

You can also use prime factorization to find the LCM of two numbers.

EXAMPLE 3

Sean and Deion both rented movies today. Sean rents a movie every 10 days. Deion rents a movie every 15 days. How many days until they rent movies on the same day again?

SOLUTION

Write the prime factorization for each number.

Identify the common prime factors (circled).

Find the LCM by finding the product of the common prime factors one time and any remaining prime factors.

LCM = 2 × 3 × 5 = 30.

$$10 \qquad 15$$
$$2 \times \boxed{5} \qquad 3 \times \boxed{5}$$
$$2 \times 3 \times 5 = 30$$

Sean and Deion will rent movies on the same day again in 30 days.

EXAMPLE 4

Ling, Kara and Sasha saw each other at the ice skating rink today. Ling goes to the rink every 2 days. Kara goes to the rink every 4 days. Sasha goes to the rink every 6 days. How many days will it be until they are together at the rink again?

SOLUTION

List multiples of each number.

2: 2, 4, 6, 8, 10, 12
4: 4, 8, 12, 16, 20, 24
6: 6, 12, 18, 24, 30, 36

Identify the LCM.

The LCM = 12

Ling, Kara and Sasha will be at the rink together in 12 days.

The least common denominator (LCD) is the least common multiple (LCM) of two or more denominators.

EXAMPLE 5

SOLUTION

Find the least common denominator of $\frac{3}{8}$ and $\frac{1}{2}$.

Identify the denominators.   8 and 2

List the multiples of both denominators.   8: $\textbf{8}$, 16, 24, 32, 40
                                              2: 2, 4, 6, $\textbf{8}$, 10, 12, 14, 16

The LCM is the LCD.

The least common denominator of $\frac{3}{8}$ and $\frac{1}{2}$ is 8.

EXERCISES

List the first five non-zero multiples for each number.

1. 2   **2.** 6   **3.** 14

Use a list of multiples to find the LCM of each set of numbers.

4. 2 and 3   **5.** 4 and 10   **6.** 3 and 12

7. 6 and 10   **8.** 3, 5 and 6   **9.** 4, 8 and 12

Use prime factorization to find the LCM of each set of numbers.

10. 4 and 6   **11.** 10 and 14   **12.** 16 and 18

13. 14 and 21   **14.** 20 and 36   **15.** 5, 15 and 20

Find the LCD of each set of fractions.

16. $\frac{1}{4}, \frac{3}{5}$ **17.** $\frac{2}{5}, \frac{3}{7}$ **18.** $\frac{7}{8}, \frac{3}{14}$

19. $\frac{2}{7}, \frac{11}{14}$ **20.** $\frac{3}{9}, \frac{9}{15}$ **21.** $\frac{7}{8}, \frac{3}{12}$

22. Chad and Mike both delivered pizza for Pizza Ritza today. Chad works every 3 days. Mike works every 4 days. How many days until Chad and Mike work together again?

23. Tristan and Hayley get their digital photos printed regularly. They saw each other on Tuesday at the store. Tristan gets her photos printed every 2 days. Hayley gets her photos printed every 5 days. On which day will Tristan and Hayley be at the store on the same day again?

24. Diego, Jordan and Scott met each other at an open gym session today. Diego goes to open gym every 4 days. Jordan goes every 5 days. Scott goes every 6 days. How many days until all three boys go to open gym session on the same day?

25. On Thursday, Matt, Ryan and Alina saw each other at the library. Matt goes to the library to study every 6 days. Ryan goes every 12 days. Alina goes every 4 days. On which day will they all be at the library at the same time?

REVIEW

Find the GCF for each pair of numbers.

26. 12 and 18

27. 15 and 45

28. 35 and 49

Use multiplication or division to find the missing number in each equivalent fraction expression.

29. $\dfrac{2}{8} = \dfrac{\square}{24}$

30. $\dfrac{7}{21} = \dfrac{\square}{3}$

31. $\dfrac{3}{5} = \dfrac{18}{\square}$

32. $\dfrac{24}{32} = \dfrac{3}{\square}$

33. $\dfrac{1}{6} = \dfrac{\square}{30}$

34. $\dfrac{27}{36} = \dfrac{3}{\square}$

Tic-Tac-Toe ~ Edible Fractions

Step 1: Start with a bag of multicolored candy (jelly beans, gum balls, gumdrops, etc.). Make sure there are at least four different colors of candy in the bag.

Step 2: Empty the candy bag. Count the total number of pieces of each color. Record how many there are of each color and the total of all colors combined.

Step 3: Write simplified fractions that represent each color as a portion of the candy.
Example: 125 pieces of red, yellow, purple or orange jelly beans

There are 45 red jelly beans.

$$\frac{\text{number of red jelly beans}}{\text{total number of candies}} = \frac{45}{125} = \frac{9}{25}$$

Step 4: Put the fractions in order from least to greatest.

ORDERING AND COMPARING FRACTIONS

 Compare fractions with like and unlike denominators to find the smallest or largest fraction.

EXPLORE!   WHICH IS LARGER?

Darin, Yolanda and Ivan finished PE class and were thirsty. Darin drank $\frac{3}{5}$ liter of water. Yolanda drank $\frac{5}{8}$ liter of water. Ivan drank $\frac{7}{12}$ liter of water.

Step 1: Use fraction tiles to model each fraction in the situation above. Draw a picture of each model.

Step 2: Explain how you can tell which student drank the most water by looking at the models.

Step 3: List the students in order from who drank the least water to who drank the most water.

Step 4: Uma ate $\frac{1}{6}$ pound of carrots. Her brother ate $\frac{2}{12}$ pound of carrots. Use the fraction tiles to determine who ate the most carrots. Explain your answer.

Step 5: Diana's hair is $\frac{5}{6}$ foot long. Mikayla's hair is $\frac{2}{3}$ foot long. Larry's hair is $\frac{7}{8}$ foot long. List the people in order from shortest hair to longest hair.

Step 6: Explain how using fraction tiles helps you order and compare fractions.

In a recent survey, three-fifths of people liked peanut butter and jam sandwiches. One-third of people liked grilled cheese. Which food is more popular?

JPD Incorporated surveyed its employees and found out that $\frac{1}{2}$ of the employees drank coffee. Tea drinkers made up $\frac{1}{6}$ of the employees. One-third of the employees preferred water. Which beverage was least popular?

In each of these problems, the fractions have different denominators. To compare fractions without using models, **the denominators of the fractions need to be equal.**

COMPARE AND ORDER FRACTIONS WITH UNLIKE DENOMINATORS

1. Find the least common denominator (LCD) for the fractions in the set.
2. Change each fraction to an equivalent fraction using the LCD.
3. Compare the numerators.

EXAMPLE 1

In a recent survey, three-fifths of the people liked peanut butter and jam. One-third liked grilled cheese sandwiches. Compare three-fifths and one-third to find which food was most popular.

SOLUTION

Convert words to numbers. $\frac{3}{5}$ and $\frac{1}{3}$

The denominators are 3 and 5.   3: 3, 6, 9, 12, ⑮
List multiples of each.   5: 5, 10, ⑮

LCM = 15

The LCM = 15, so the LCD = 15.

Make equivalent fractions with denominators of 15.

$\frac{3}{5} = \frac{9}{15}$ (×3, ×3) $\frac{1}{3} = \frac{5}{15}$ (×5, ×5)

Compare the numerators.
Nine is larger than 5.

$\frac{9}{15} > \frac{5}{15}$

> means "greater than"
< means "less than"

Substitute the original fractions in the comparison.

If $\frac{9}{15} > \frac{5}{15}$, then $\frac{3}{5} > \frac{1}{3}$.

The group that liked peanut butter and jam sandwiches was larger.

EXAMPLE 2

List the following fractions from least to greatest: $\frac{1}{2}, \frac{1}{6}, \frac{1}{3}$.

SOLUTION

List the fractions that need to be compared. $\frac{1}{2}, \frac{1}{6}, \frac{1}{3}$

The denominators are 2, 6 and 3.   2: 2, 4, ⑥ 8
List multiples of each.   3: 3, ⑥ 9
                                                          6: ⑥ 12, 18

The LCM = 6, so the LCD = 6

Make equivalent fractions.

$\frac{1}{2} = \frac{3}{6}$ (×3, ×3) $\frac{1}{3} = \frac{2}{6}$ (×2, ×2)

Compare numerators and put them in order from least to greatest.

$\frac{1}{6} < \frac{2}{6} < \frac{3}{6}$

Substitute the original fractions for each simplified fraction to answer the question.

$\frac{1}{6}, \frac{1}{3}, \frac{1}{2}$

EXAMPLE 3

Find a fraction between $\frac{1}{6}$ and $\frac{1}{2}$. Write in simplest form.

SOLUTION

The denominators are 6 and 2.

$$\frac{1}{6}, \frac{1}{2}$$

List multiples of each denominator.

2: 2, 4, ⑥, 8
6: ⑥, 12, 18

The LCM = 6, so the LCD = 6

Make equivalent fractions.

$$\xrightarrow{\times 3}$$
$$\frac{1}{2} = \frac{3}{6}$$
$$\xrightarrow{\times 3}$$

Compare the fractions.

$$\frac{1}{6} < \frac{3}{6}$$

Write a fraction that goes between the two fractions.

$\frac{2}{6}$ would go between $\frac{1}{6}$ and $\frac{3}{6}$

Write the fraction in simplest form.

$$\frac{2}{6} = \frac{1}{3}$$

> Don't forget that all answers should be written in simplest form.

EXERCISES

Write the fraction for each drawing. Circle the largest fraction in each pair.

1.

2.

Compare each pair of fractions. Replace each ⬤ with <, > or = to make a true sentence.

3. $\frac{3}{5}$ ⬤ $\frac{3}{4}$

4. $\frac{5}{8}$ ⬤ $\frac{2}{3}$

5. $\frac{3}{12}$ ⬤ $\frac{6}{24}$

6. $\frac{3}{10}$ ⬤ $\frac{1}{4}$

7. $\frac{5}{12}$ ⬤ $\frac{2}{5}$

8. $\frac{5}{7}$ ⬤ $\frac{3}{5}$

9. $\frac{1}{4}$ ⬤ $\frac{1}{3}$

10. $\frac{3}{5}$ ⬤ $\frac{7}{12}$

11. $\frac{6}{11}$ ⬤ $\frac{1}{2}$

Write each set of fractions in order from least to greatest.

12. $\frac{1}{2}, \frac{3}{4}, \frac{1}{4}$

13. $\frac{2}{5}, \frac{1}{3}, \frac{1}{5}$

14. $\frac{3}{8}, \frac{5}{8}, \frac{1}{2}$

15. $\frac{3}{10}, \frac{2}{5}, \frac{7}{10}$

16. $\frac{5}{6}, \frac{2}{6}, \frac{1}{4}$

17. $\frac{11}{15}, \frac{1}{3}, \frac{4}{5}$

Find a fraction between each pair of fractions. Write in simplest form.

18. $\frac{1}{3}, \frac{5}{8}$

19. $\frac{1}{3}, \frac{4}{5}$

20. $\frac{3}{8}, \frac{3}{5}$

21. $\frac{2}{9}, \frac{3}{7}$

22. $\frac{1}{5}, \frac{1}{3}$

23. $\frac{4}{9}, \frac{2}{3}$

24. Hani was making a cake that called for $\frac{5}{8}$ cup of cocoa and $\frac{2}{3}$ cup of butter. Would he need more cocoa or butter?

25. Worker honey bees are approximately $\frac{2}{3}$ inch long. Drone honey bees are approximately $\frac{1}{6}$ inch long. Which are longer?

26. Cody dumped out a box of gum balls. Two-ninths of the gum balls were pink. One-third of the gum balls were green. Four-ninths of the gum balls were white.
   a. Put the fractions in order from least to greatest.
   b. Cody had the most of which color of gum ball?

27. Kabira bought three candles that were the same size. After a few weeks she noticed she had burned the yellow candle $\frac{5}{12}$ of the way down. The red candle had burned $\frac{1}{3}$ of the way. The green candle had burned down $\frac{3}{8}$ of the way. Which candle had burned down the most?

REVIEW

Find the LCM for each pair of numbers.

28. 6 and 8

29. 12 and 15

30. 9 and 5

Use multiplication or division to find the missing number in each equivalent fraction expression.

31. $\frac{4}{7} = \frac{16}{\square}$

32. $\frac{15}{19} = \frac{\square}{38}$

33. $\frac{25}{60} = \frac{5}{\square}$

34. $\frac{35}{56} = \frac{\square}{8}$

Write each fraction in simplest form. If it is already in simplest form, write *simplest form*.

35. $\dfrac{3}{30}$

36. $\dfrac{12}{14}$

37. $\dfrac{26}{31}$

38. $\dfrac{42}{70}$

Tic-Tac-Toe ~ Favorites

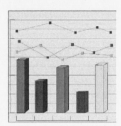

Step 1: Create a survey question and four options by filling in the blanks:

What is your favorite _____?

Option 1:_____

Option 2:_____

Option 3:_____

Option 4:_____

Step 2: Survey at least fifty people and record their answers.

Step 3: Create a bar graph to show your results.

Step 4: Write the results for each option as simplified fractions.

Example: What is your favorite color?

Option 1: Red $\dfrac{20 \text{ people}}{50 \text{ people}} = \dfrac{2}{5}$

Step 5: Order the fractions from least to greatest.

Step 6: Write a paragraph summarizing the results of the survey.

Step 7: Create a poster using **Steps 1-6** to display your process.

MIXED NUMBERS AND IMPROPER FRACTIONS

LESSON 6

Write improper fractions as mixed numbers.
Write mixed numbers as improper fractions.

A proper fraction has a numerator that is less than the denominator.

$\frac{9}{10}$ (nine-tenths) $\frac{2}{3}$ (two-thirds)

An improper fraction has a numerator that is equal to or greater than the denominator.

$\frac{11}{10}$ (eleven-tenths) $\frac{4}{3}$ (four-thirds)

A mixed number is the sum of a whole number and a fraction.

$1\frac{1}{10}$ (one and one-tenth) $1\frac{1}{3}$ (one and one-third)

A number line can help compare improper fractions to mixed numbers.

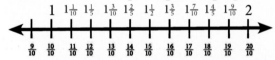   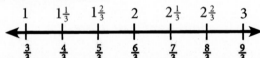

REWRITING IMPROPER FRACTIONS AS MIXED NUMBERS

1. Divide the numerator by the denominator. The quotient is the whole number in the mixed number.
2. Write the remainder as the numerator over the original denominator. This is the fraction in the mixed number.

EXAMPLE 1   **Change the improper fraction $\frac{14}{4}$ to a mixed number.**

SOLUTION   Divide the numerator by the denominator.
The quotient is the whole number.
The remainder goes over the original
denominator to make the fraction.

Simplify.

$$3\frac{2}{4} = 3\frac{1}{2}$$

26 *Lesson 6 ~ Mixed Numbers And Improper Fractions*

REWRITING MIXED NUMBERS AS IMPROPER FRACTION

1. Multiply the whole number by the denominator.
2. Add the numerator to the product.
3. Write this number as the numerator and keep the original denominator as the denominator of the improper fraction.

EXAMPLE 2

Change the mixed number $2\frac{3}{4}$ to an improper fraction.

SOLUTION

Multiply the whole number by the denominator. Add the numerator to the product.

$$2\frac{3}{4} = \frac{4 \times 2 + 3}{4} = \frac{11}{4}$$

This number becomes the numerator. The denominator stays the same.

$$\frac{11}{4} = 2\frac{3}{4}$$

EXPLORE!   **CHOCOLATE CHIP COOKIES**

Lynn got out a recipe for cookies. She was confused when she looked at the amounts. The entire recipe was written with fractions. Most of them were improper fractions. Help her simplify the recipe by creating a new recipe card.

> **Chocolate Chip Cookies**
>
> $\frac{9}{8}$ cups butter $\frac{19}{8}$ cups flour
>
> $\frac{6}{8}$ cup sugar $\frac{5}{4}$ tsp. baking soda
>
> $\frac{6}{8}$ cup brown sugar $\frac{9}{8}$ tsp. salt
>
> $\frac{8}{4}$ eggs $\frac{18}{8}$ cups chocolate chips
>
> $\frac{10}{8}$ tsp. vanilla

Step 1: Look at the amount of butter on the recipe card. Draw a model of this fraction on paper. Write it as a mixed number on a blank recipe card.

Step 2: Draw the fraction that represents the amount of sugar in the cookies on your paper. Write it as a simplified fraction on the new recipe card.

Step 3: Continue to use the drawings to figure out the mixed number, whole number or simplified fraction for each ingredient. Draw each of these fractions on your paper and record the fraction, whole number or mixed number on your recipe card.

Step 4: Lynn wanted to confuse her brother by changing a recipe for brownies into improper, non-simplified fractions. Create a recipe card from the brownie recipe below to confuse him.

Brownies			
$\frac{1}{2}$ cup butter	$\frac{1}{4}$ cup sugar	2 eggs	$1\frac{1}{2}$ tsp. vanilla
$\frac{1}{3}$ cup unsweetened cocoa	$1\frac{1}{8}$ cups flour	$\frac{1}{4}$ tsp. salt	$\frac{3}{8}$ tsp. baking powder

EXERCISES

Write a mixed number and improper fraction that represents the shaded amount for each drawing.

1.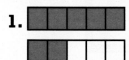

2.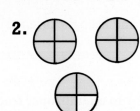

3.

Write each improper fraction as a mixed number in simplest form.

4. $\dfrac{9}{2}$

5. $\dfrac{7}{3}$

6. $\dfrac{24}{5}$

7. $\dfrac{20}{6}$

8. $\dfrac{22}{9}$

9. $\dfrac{32}{7}$

10. $\dfrac{5}{2}$

11. $\dfrac{40}{12}$

12. $\dfrac{44}{14}$

13. The world's largest functioning mobile phone is the Maxi Mobile, according to the Guinness Book of World Records. It measures $\frac{336}{50}$ feet tall. Write this improper fraction as a mixed number in simplest form.

14. The average weight of a newborn baby is $\frac{117}{16}$ pounds. Write this improper fraction as a mixed number.

Write each mixed number as an improper fraction.

15. $4\frac{2}{3}$

16. $1\frac{5}{6}$

17. $2\frac{4}{7}$

18. $3\frac{3}{5}$

19. $5\frac{1}{8}$

20 $4\frac{3}{10}$

21. $6\frac{3}{9}$

22. $8\frac{1}{2}$

23. $3\frac{9}{15}$

24. According to the Guinness Book of World Records, the world's longest skateboard measured $30\frac{1}{12}$ feet long. Write this mixed number as an improper fraction.

Write each set of improper fractions and mixed numbers in order from least to greatest.

25. $\dfrac{7}{2}$, $3\frac{1}{4}$, $\dfrac{9}{2}$

26. $\dfrac{8}{3}$, $2\frac{1}{6}$, $\dfrac{10}{3}$

27. $\dfrac{7}{4}$, $1\frac{1}{8}$, $\dfrac{3}{2}$

28. Your class is planning an ice cream party. There are 6 ice cream bars in each box. There are 23 students in your class. Each student will eat 1 ice cream bar. Write how many boxes of ice cream bars your class will eat as a mixed number.

29. Which is longer, $10\frac{5}{8}$ inches or $\frac{40}{4}$ inches?

30. It rained $1\frac{7}{8}$ inches on Monday. On Tuesday, it rained $\frac{7}{4}$ of an inches. On which day did it rain more?

REVIEW

Find the LCD of each pair of fractions.

31. $\frac{1}{5}, \frac{2}{3}$

32. $\frac{3}{8}, \frac{7}{12}$

33. $\frac{4}{10}, \frac{5}{8}$

Compare each pair of fractions. Replace each ⬤ **with <, > or = to make a true sentence.**

34. $\frac{5}{7}$ ⬤ $\frac{3}{4}$

35. $\frac{2}{3}$ ⬤ $\frac{2}{5}$

36. $\frac{4}{10}$ ⬤ $\frac{6}{15}$

Find the GCF of each pair of numbers.

37. 36 and 18

38. 8 and 16

39. 10 and 55

TIC-TAC-TOE ~ RECIPE MIX-UP

Choose six of your favorite recipes. Each recipe must have a minimum of five ingredients.

Change all of the numbers and fractions in the recipe by using an equivalent fraction for each fraction given. Write all mixed numbers as improper fractions.

Examples: "2 cups flour" can be written as "$\frac{10}{5}$ cups flour"
"$\frac{3}{4}$ cup brown sugar" can be written as "$\frac{9}{12}$ cup brown sugar"
"$1\frac{1}{2}$ tsp. salt" can be written as "$\frac{3}{2}$ tsp. salt"

Create a "My Favorite Recipes" cookbook using the recipes with mixed-up fractions. Include directions with each recipe.

MEASURING IN INCHES

Use a customary ruler to measure inches and fractions of an inch.

A jumbo paper clip is about $\frac{7}{8}$ inch long.

A pen is about $5\frac{1}{2}$ inches long.

A pencil sharpener is about $1\frac{1}{4}$ inches long.

In many careers it is important to know how to measure accurately using a ruler. A carpet installer needs to know the length and width of a room to order the correct amount of carpet. A builder needs to measure wooden beams so they are the same length. A plumber needs to measure the length of pipe accurately. A ruler measures inches using different sized denominators like the examples above. It is important to know what each line on a ruler represents.

A foot-long ruler has 12 inches. Each inch is separated into sixteenths (16ths) on the ruler using different sized lines, called tick marks. There are 16 equally divided spaces between every inch on a ruler.

EXPLORE!   USING A CUSTOMARY RULER

Step 1: Copy and complete the table below by writing each fraction in simplest form.

Tick Mark	1	2	3	4	5	6	7	8	9	10	11	12	13	14	15	16
Fraction of Inch	$\frac{1}{16}$	$\frac{2}{16}$	$\frac{3}{16}$	$\frac{4}{16}$	$\frac{5}{16}$											
Simplest Form																

Step 2: How many fractions in the table above simplify to a whole number? What do you notice about the tick mark(s) on the ruler that correspond to the measurement(s) that are whole numbers?

Step 3: After simplifying the fractions, how many fractions have a 2 in the denominator? What do you notice about the tick marks on the ruler that correspond to the measurements with a 2 in the denominator?

Step 4: How many of the simplified fractions have a 4 in the denominator? What do you notice about the tick marks on the ruler that correspond to the measurements with a 4 in the denominator?

Step 5: How many fractions have an 8 in the denominator? What do you notice about the tick marks on the ruler that correspond to the measurements with an 8 the denominator?

Step 6: After simplifying the fractions, how many fractions have a 16 in the denominator? What do you notice about the tick marks on the ruler that correspond to the measurements with a 16 in the denominator?

It is important to measure accurately when measuring the length of a wall in a room or the height of a person at the doctor's office. To measure length as accurately as possible, measure to the nearest sixteenth of an inch.

MEASURING WITH A CUSTOMARY RULER

1. Locate the tick mark that most closely matches the length of the object.
2. Record the whole number of inches.
3. Record the fractional part of an inch that the tick mark represents.
4. Write the whole number of inches with the fraction part of an inch in simplest form.

EXAMPLE 1

Measure each line using inches on a ruler. Measure to the nearest 16th of an inch.

a. ──────────────────────

b. ──────────────

SOLUTIONS

For both measurements, line the "0" inch mark of the ruler with the left edge of the line drawn. Identify which tick mark on the ruler corresponds to the right end of the line.

a.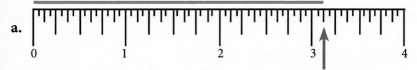

The line corresponds to 3 whole inches plus 2 additional tick marks.

$$3 + \frac{2}{16} = 3\frac{2}{16}$$

Write the fraction in simplest form. $3\frac{2}{16} = 3\frac{1}{8}$ inches

b.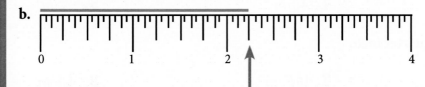

The line corresponds to 2 whole inches plus 4 additional tick marks.

$$2 + \frac{4}{16} = 2\frac{4}{16}$$

Write the fraction in simplest form. $2\frac{4}{16} = 2\frac{1}{4}$ inches.

Sometimes measurements will be rounded to the nearest quarter ($\frac{1}{4}$) inch or half ($\frac{1}{2}$) inch when exact answers are not required.

EXAMPLE 2

Measure the line to the nearest quarter inch.

_____

SOLUTION

Measuring to the nearest quarter inch means the answer could include
$\frac{1}{4}$ inch, $\frac{2}{4}$ inch, $\frac{3}{4}$ inch, or $\frac{4}{4}$ inch

> Notice: $\frac{2}{4} = \frac{1}{2}$
> and $\frac{4}{4} = 1$

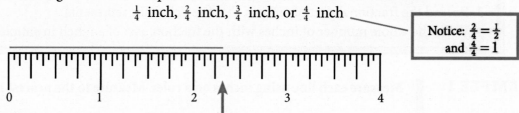

Use a ruler to see that the line is 2 inches and then ends closer to the $\frac{1}{4}$ tick mark than to the $\frac{1}{2}$ tick mark.

The line is about $2\frac{1}{4}$ inches long.

EXERCISES

1. The tick marks divide each inch into how many sections?

2. How many inches are in 1 foot?

Round to the nearest half inch.

3. $3\frac{1}{16}$ in

4. $4\frac{5}{8}$ in

5. $9\frac{7}{8}$ in

Round to the nearest quarter inch.

6. $2\frac{3}{16}$ in

7. $10\frac{15}{16}$ in

8. $4\frac{7}{16}$ in

Measure the length of each line to the nearest sixteenth of an inch.

9. _____

10. _____

11. _____

12. _____

Measure the length of each line to the nearest quarter of an inch.

13. _____

14. _____

15. _____

16. Kim and Marci measured the width of the table they sat at each day at school. The width of the table was $25\frac{9}{16}$ inches. The math teacher asked the students to measure the width of the table to the nearest quarter inch. Kim answered $25\frac{3}{4}$ inches. Marci insisted the answer was $25\frac{1}{2}$ inches.

    a. Which answer is closest to $25\frac{9}{16}$ inches?

    b. Kim was sure the answer could not end in $\frac{1}{2}$ if they were supposed to round to the nearest quarter inch. Explain why the answer can or cannot end in $\frac{1}{2}$ when rounding to the nearest quarter inch.

Draw a line that has the given length.

17. $\frac{3}{8}$ inch

18. $5\frac{1}{4}$ inches

19. $2\frac{1}{2}$ inches

20. $3\frac{9}{16}$ inches

21. 4 inches

Determine which measurement is longer.

22. $\frac{1}{8}$ inch or $\frac{1}{4}$ inch

23. $\frac{1}{2}$ inch or $\frac{7}{16}$ inch

24. $\frac{5}{8}$ inch or $\frac{3}{4}$ inch

25. Jon had three wires. The red wire was $\frac{1}{4}$ inch long. The blue wire was $\frac{3}{8}$ inch long. The green wire was $\frac{3}{12}$ inch long. Which two wires are equal in length?

26. Martina has a piece of purple yarn that is $3\frac{1}{2}$ inches long. She has a piece of yellow yarn that is $3\frac{7}{12}$ inches long. Which piece of yarn is longer?

27. Antonio measured his hand from his wrist to the tip of his longest finger. It was $7\frac{3}{4}$ inches long. His brother's hand measured $7\frac{7}{8}$ inches long.

    a. Whose hand length is shortest?

    b. Measure the length of your hand. Is it longer or shorter than Antonio's hand?

REVIEW

Write each set of fractions in order from least to greatest.

28. $\frac{1}{2}, \frac{3}{16}, \frac{7}{16}$

29. $\frac{4}{5}, \frac{7}{10}, \frac{2}{5}$

30. $\frac{7}{9}, \frac{11}{18}, \frac{20}{27}$

Write each improper fraction as a mixed number.

31. $\frac{17}{9}$

32. $\frac{16}{5}$

33. $\frac{9}{4}$

TIC-TAC-TOE ~ COINS AND FRACTIONS

A coin can be written as a fraction of a dollar.

Example: A fifty cent piece.

There are 50 cents in one fifty cent piece and one hundred cents in a dollar.

One fifty cent piece is $\dfrac{50 \text{ cents}}{100 \text{ cents}} = \dfrac{50}{100} = \dfrac{1}{2}$ of a dollar.

This makes sense because a fifty cent piece is one half of a dollar.

Step 1: Copy and complete the first five rows on the table below to show the value of each coin as a fraction of a dollar. Add 10 blank rows to the table.

Coin	Value as a fraction
Fifty cent piece	$\frac{1}{2}$ of a dollar
Quarter	
Dime	
Nickel	
Penny	

Step 2: Put 9 quarters, 9 dimes, 9 nickels, and 9 pennies into a bag. Reach into the bag and pull out 3 coins. Record the coins in the first empty row on your table. Figure out the combined value as a fraction. Write the fraction, in simplest form, in the table.

   Example: 1 quarter, 2 pennies is $\frac{27}{100}$ of a dollar.

Step 3: Put the coins back into the bag. Reach in and pull out 3-8 coins. Record these coins in another row on your table. Figure out the combined value as in **Step 2**.

Step 4: Repeat **Step 3** until you have completed ten more rows on the table.

Step 5: Write a quiz with at least ten questions about fractions of a dollar. Make at least half of your questions challenging.

   Example: "Which three coins can be combined to make $\frac{40}{100}$ of a dollar?"

   This question could be more challenging by simplifying the fraction in the question. Change the question to, "Which three coins could be combined to make $\frac{2}{5}$ of a dollar?"

Step 6: Make an answer key for your quiz.

Vocabulary

composite number	improper fraction	prime factorization
equivalent fractions	least common denominator	prime number
factor	least common multiple	proper fraction
fraction	mixed number	tick marks
greatest common factor	multiple	simplest form

Find the greatest common factor (GFC) of a set of numbers.
Write equivalent fractions.
Write fractions in simplest form.
Find the least common multiple for a set of numbers.
Find the least common denominator for a set of fractions.
Compare fractions with like and unlike denominators to find the smallest or largest fraction.
Write improper fractions as mixed numbers.
Write mixed numbers as improper fractions.
Use a customary ruler to measure inches and fractions of an inch.

Lesson 1 ~ Greatest Common Factor
• •
List the factors of each number. State whether each number is prime or composite.

1. 5

2. 9

3. 21

Find the greatest common factor (GCF) for each pair of numbers.

4. 15 and 20

5. 14 and 21

6. 12 and 30

7. 18 and 27

8. 10 and 25

9. 40 and 56

Lesson 2 ~ Equivalent Fractions
• •
Use models to show whether or not each pair of fractions is equivalent.

10. $\frac{1}{4}$ and $\frac{2}{8}$

11. $\frac{3}{8}$ and $\frac{5}{6}$

Use multiplication or division to find the missing number in each equivalent fraction expression.

12. $\frac{5}{9} = \frac{\square}{45}$

13. $\frac{1}{2} = \frac{4}{\square}$

14. $\frac{12}{36} = \frac{\square}{6}$

15. $\frac{3}{7} = \frac{21}{\square}$

16. $\frac{14}{56} = \frac{1}{\square}$

17. $\frac{18}{20} = \frac{\square}{10}$

Write two fractions that are equivalent to each fraction.

18. $\dfrac{3}{9}$

19. $\dfrac{6}{10}$

20. $\dfrac{1}{2}$

Lesson 3 ~ Simplifying Fractions

• •

Write each fraction in simplest form. If it is already in simplest form, write *simplest form*.

21. $\dfrac{9}{12}$

22. $\dfrac{11}{15}$

23. $\dfrac{12}{15}$

24. $\dfrac{20}{30}$

25. $\dfrac{24}{81}$

26. $\dfrac{20}{37}$

27. Peter's dirt bike weighs $\frac{22}{200}$ ton. Simplify this measurement.

Write each fraction in simplest form. Tell whether or not the pair of fractions is equivalent.

28. $\dfrac{20}{35}$ and $\dfrac{8}{14}$

29. $\dfrac{12}{30}$ and $\dfrac{24}{50}$

Lesson 4 ~ Least Common Multiple

• •

List the first five nonzero multiples for each number.

30. 3

31. 15

32. 10

Find the least common multiple (LCM) of each set of numbers.

33. 8 and 20

34. 9 and 12

35. 32 and 24

Find the least common denominator (LCD) of each set of fractions.

36. $\dfrac{5}{25}, \dfrac{2}{10}$

37. $\dfrac{3}{8}, \dfrac{5}{12}$

38. $\dfrac{4}{11}, \dfrac{2}{4}$

39. The Piper and Roy families like to hike on the Oregon Coast. Both families went hiking today. Mr. Piper told Mr. Roy that the Piper family goes hiking every 15 days. Mr. Roy said his family goes hiking every 10 days. How many days until both families go hiking again on the same day?

Replace each ● with <, > or = to make a true sentence.

40. $\frac{5}{6}$ ● $\frac{9}{10}$

41. $\frac{4}{15}$ ● $\frac{1}{6}$

42. $\frac{3}{4}$ ● $\frac{12}{18}$

Write each set of fractions in order from least to greatest.

43. $\frac{2}{5}, \frac{3}{10}, \frac{3}{5}$

44. $\frac{1}{4}, \frac{3}{4}, \frac{2}{3}$

45. $\frac{4}{5}, \frac{3}{7}, \frac{2}{5}$

46. Levi had a candy bar. He ate $\frac{3}{8}$ of it. His sister ate $\frac{5}{16}$ of it. Who ate less?

47. Hoi read $\frac{7}{15}$ of her book on Monday. She read $\frac{4}{9}$ of her book on Tuesday. On which day did she read more of her book?

Lesson 6 ~ Mixed Numbers and Improper Fractions

Write each mixed number as an improper fraction.

48. $3\frac{5}{6}$

49. $2\frac{7}{11}$

50. $7\frac{5}{12}$

Write each improper fraction as a mixed number.

51. $\frac{7}{2}$

52. $\frac{23}{5}$

53. $\frac{34}{11}$

Write each set of improper fractions and mixed numbers in order from least to greatest.

54. $2\frac{1}{10}, \frac{11}{10}, 2\frac{3}{5}$

55. $1\frac{1}{3}, \frac{11}{6}, \frac{5}{3}$

56. $3\frac{1}{8}, \frac{17}{8}, \frac{7}{2}$

Lesson 7 ~ Measuring In Inches

Measure the length of each line to the nearest eighth of an inch.

57. ⎯⎯⎯⎯⎯⎯⎯⎯⎯⎯⎯⎯⎯⎯⎯⎯⎯⎯⎯⎯⎯⎯⎯⎯⎯

58. ⎯⎯⎯⎯⎯⎯⎯⎯⎯⎯⎯⎯⎯⎯⎯⎯⎯

59. ⎯⎯⎯⎯⎯⎯⎯⎯⎯⎯⎯⎯⎯⎯⎯⎯⎯⎯⎯⎯

Measure the length of each line to the nearest quarter of an inch.

60. _____

61. _____

62. _____

Draw a line that has the given length.

63. $5\frac{1}{8}$ inches

64. $3\frac{1}{2}$ inches

65. $\frac{7}{16}$ inch

66. $2\frac{3}{4}$ inches

TIC-TAC-TOE ~ CONCAVE AND CONVEX

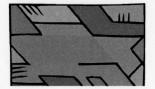 A concave figure is a closed figure that has an indentation.

A convex figure is a closed figure with no indentation.

Step 1: Draw seven different line segments with the following lengths onto a piece of paper. Leave room to cut each of them out.

   a. $2\frac{7}{8}$ inches   **b.** $1\frac{1}{4}$ inches   **c.** $\dfrac{15}{16}$ inches

   d. $3\frac{1}{2}$ inches   **e.** $1\frac{13}{16}$ inches   **f.** $2\frac{5}{8}$ inches   **g.** $4\frac{3}{16}$ inches

Step 2: Cut each line segment out carefully.

Step 3: Manipulate the seven cut-out line segments to create a concave figure. Sketch this figure onto a piece of paper. Label the lengths of each side.

Step 4: Repeat **Step 3** until you have three or more concave figures.

Step 5: Manipulate the seven cut-out line segments to create a convex figure. Sketch this figure onto a piece of paper. Label the lengths of each side.

Step 6: Repeat **Step 5** until you have three or more convex figures.

CAREER FOCUS

DIXIE
METALSMITH
LINCOLN CITY, OREGON

I am a metalsmith. I work as an artist making pieces for art galleries and for sale. I design jewelry and also teach metal-working to children ages nine to thirteen at a community center and at an arts camp. Sometimes I work with a wood artist as well to design pieces that have both metal and wood in them.

My job requires many different skills. The first thing I must do is put my drawings on graph paper. When I am working with another artist, they will also put their designs on graph paper. We then use scale and proportion to determine how big to make our actual piece. When I work with metal I use millimeters to measure my designs. Artists who work with wood might use a bigger measurement such as inches. Getting accurate measurements is very important when making my designs. When I am working with somebody else, we have to make sure that our measurements match up perfectly for the final piece.

I also make jewelry. In making jewelry there are many formulas I must use, including determining ring sizes using circumference. When making jewelry I often have to carve a piece in wax first. I can then use formulas to calculate the amount of metal I will need to make the project. Formulas also help to determine what kind of alloy to use, how big the setting needs to be and many other things that go into getting a finished piece of jewelry.

Jewelers and metalsmiths come from many different backgrounds. I have a degree in Art Education and also served an apprenticeship in a small jewelry/sculpture foundry. After that, I went to work in several other foundries. Other metalsmiths may choose to get training through a technical school or distance learning class.

Salaries can vary in the jewelry field, but usually start at $8.00 - $15.00 an hour. With two years of experience in Portland, a jeweler can make $16.00 - $25.00 an hour, depending on expertise. There are jobs in small businesses and larger manufacturing situations. In the Portland area the median salary for that type of job is $34,000 per year. About forty percent of all jewelers are self-employed, so there are many opportunities to earn different amounts.

I love this profession because of all the skills it requires from design to completion. I also like the business aspects of figuring costs, overhead and sales. There is always more to learn and many challenges. Teaching provides an opportunity to pass on my knowledge and giving students tools to express their ideas. My work with another artist gives me new direction and inspiration for growing in my profession.

BLOCK 2 ~ FRACTIONS AND DECIMALS
ADDING AND SUBTRACTING FRACTIONS

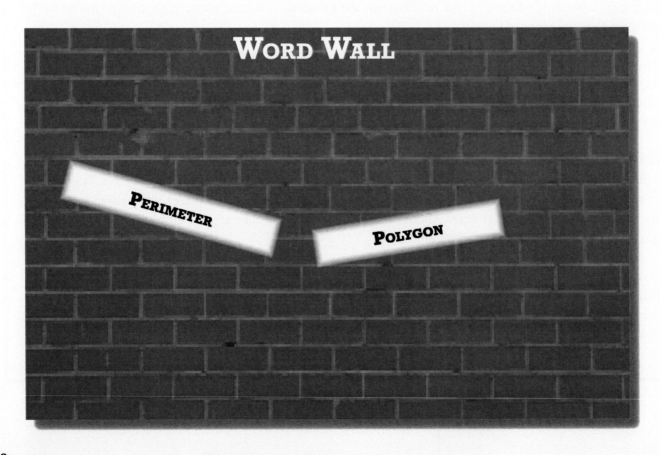

BLOCK 2 ~ ADDING AND SUBTRACTING FRACTIONS

TIC - TAC - TOE

ESTIMATION RAP

Write a rap song about situations where estimating is acceptable and where estimating would cause disasters.

See page 45 for details.

MEASURE THE PERIMETER

Measure the length and width of several different frames at home or at a store. Find each perimeter.

See page 63 for details.

CREATE THE PROBLEM

Write problems using pairs of fractions that add up to a given sum.

See page 59 for details.

MODELS

Create a brochure to teach how to add and subtract fractions using models.

See page 50 for details.

FIND THE SUM

Find the sum of problems of three or more fractions with different denominators.

$$\frac{1}{2} + \frac{1}{3} + \frac{1}{4}$$

See page 66 for details.

LIGHTS, CAMERA, ACTION

Create a skit where characters use addition or subtraction of fractions to solve their problem.

See page 54 for details.

TRIATHLON

Find different distances using Oregon triathlon races.

See page 55 for details.

INTERVIEW

Interview someone who uses fractions. Report on how that person uses fractions.

See page 45 for details.

YOU ARE THE AUTHOR

Investigate children's books on fractions. Write your own children's book.

See page 54 for details.

ESTIMATING SUMS AND DIFFERENCES

 Estimate sums and differences of expressions with fractions and mixed numbers.

A teacher needed two boxes of pencils. Hayden said he had $\frac{1}{6}$ of a box at home. Trevor thought he had $\frac{2}{5}$ of a box. Kelsey knew she had $\frac{4}{7}$ of a box at home. Asha thought she had $\frac{5}{6}$ of a box. The students were not sure if they had enough pencils to help the teacher reach two boxes.

Estimating could help these students get a good idea of whether or not they had enough pencils.

ESTIMATING SUMS OR DIFFERENCES USING FRACTIONS

1. Round to 0, $\frac{1}{2}$ or 1, whichever is closest.
   - If the numerator is very small compared to the denominator, estimate as 0.
   - If the numerator is about half of the denominator, estimate as $\frac{1}{2}$.
   - If the numerator is nearly as big as the denominator, estimate as 1.
2. Add or subtract.

EXAMPLE 1

Hayden had about $\frac{1}{6}$ of a box of pencils. Trevor had about $\frac{2}{5}$ of a box. Kelsey had about $\frac{4}{7}$ of a box and Asha had about $\frac{5}{6}$ of a box. About how many boxes of pencils do they have altogether?

SOLUTION

Compare each numerator to its denominator to determine the estimated value.

Hayden	Trevor	Kelsey	Asha
$\frac{1}{6} \rightarrow 0$	$\frac{2}{5} \rightarrow \frac{1}{2}$	$\frac{4}{7} \rightarrow \frac{1}{2}$	$\frac{5}{6} \rightarrow 1$
The numerator is very small compared to the denominator.	The numerators are about half of their denominators.		The numerator is nearly as big as the denominator.

Add the estimated amounts.

$$0 + \frac{1}{2} + \frac{1}{2} + 1 = 2$$

They have about two boxes of pencils among the four of them.

$$\frac{1}{6} + \frac{2}{5} + \frac{4}{7} + \frac{5}{6} \approx 2$$

The $\approx$ sign means "about" or "approximately."

EXAMPLE 2

Asha found that, instead of $\frac{5}{6}$ of a box of pencils, she had $\frac{4}{9}$ of a box. About how much less does she have than she originally thought?

SOLUTION

Write the problem. $\frac{5}{6} - \frac{4}{9} \approx$

Round to 0, $\frac{1}{2}$ or 1. $1 - \frac{1}{2}$

Subtract. $1 - \frac{1}{2} = \frac{1}{2}$ so $\frac{5}{6} - \frac{4}{9} \approx \frac{1}{2}$

Asha has about half of a box less than she thought she had.

ESTIMATING SUMS OR DIFFERENCES USING MIXED NUMBERS

1. Round to the nearest whole number
2. Add or subtract.

EXAMPLE 3

Estimate the value of $2\frac{1}{3} + 5\frac{6}{7}$.

SOLUTION

Write the problem. $2\frac{1}{3} + 5\frac{6}{7}$

Round to the nearest
whole number. $2 + 6$

Add. $2 + 6 = 8$

$2\frac{1}{3} + 5\frac{6}{7} \approx 8$

EXAMPLE 4

According to the Guinness Book of World Records, the world's tallest man, Robert Pershing Wadlow, was $8\frac{11}{12}$ feet tall. The world's shortest woman, Zhu Haizhen, was $2\frac{7}{12}$ feet tall. Approximately how much taller was the tallest man than the shortest woman?

SOLUTION

Write the problem. $8\frac{11}{12} - 2\frac{7}{12} \approx$

Round to the nearest whole number. $9 - 3$

Subtract. $9 - 3 = 6$

$8\frac{11}{12} - 2\frac{7}{12} \approx 6$

The tallest man was about six feet taller than the shortest woman.

EXERCISES

Estimate each sum or difference.

1. $\dfrac{2}{3}+\dfrac{2}{11}$

2. $\dfrac{3}{5}+\dfrac{4}{9}$

3. $\dfrac{9}{10}-\dfrac{7}{8}$

4. $\dfrac{8}{15}+\dfrac{6}{7}$

5. $\dfrac{32}{37}+\dfrac{21}{25}$

6. $\dfrac{7}{9}-\dfrac{6}{13}$

7. $\dfrac{19}{21}-\dfrac{1}{9}$

8. $\dfrac{8}{15}-\dfrac{10}{21}$

9. $\dfrac{9}{19}+\dfrac{2}{15}$

10. Melanie exercised for $\frac{7}{8}$ hour on Saturday. On Sunday she exercised for $\frac{3}{5}$ hour. About how many hours did Melanie exercise in the two days?

11. Sapphire and Rebekah each brought a pie to a family party. Sapphire cut her pie into 12 pieces. After the party, $\frac{1}{12}$ of the pie was left. Rebekah cut her pie into 8 pieces. She had $\frac{5}{8}$ of the pie left after the party. About how much more of Rebekah's pie was left than Sapphire's pie?

12. Nigel told his mom he completed $\frac{1}{10}$ of the family's chores. His brother, Nick, completed $\frac{4}{9}$ of the chores. Estimate what fraction of the chores were completed altogether.

Estimate each sum or difference.

13. $2\frac{2}{7}+5\frac{8}{9}$

14. $2\frac{1}{5}+3\frac{4}{7}$

15. $6\frac{8}{13}+8\frac{3}{4}$

16. $9\frac{1}{2}+1\frac{1}{3}$

17. $11\frac{2}{3}+12\frac{7}{8}$

18. $6\frac{13}{14}-4\frac{1}{8}$

19. $4\frac{8}{9}-1\frac{3}{5}$

20. $5\frac{2}{5}-2\frac{6}{11}$

21. $9\frac{2}{9}-3\frac{7}{8}$

22. After soccer practice, Jaafan drank $1\frac{7}{8}$ cups of water. His friend, Brock, drank $1\frac{1}{7}$ cups of water. Approximately how much more water did Jaafan drink than Brock?

23. Trey's family drove from Redmond to Madras. The map showed that they had traveled $26\frac{3}{20}$ miles. They drove on to Warm Springs which was another $14\frac{4}{5}$ miles. Estimate the total number of miles they traveled from Redmond to Warm Springs.

24. Lacey made bread. The recipe called for $2\frac{3}{4}$ cups of flour at the beginning. She added an additional $3\frac{1}{6}$ cups of flour after mixing the first ingredients. Estimate how many total cups of flour Lacey needed to make the bread.

25. When the Jacobsens designed their house, one room was $16\frac{1}{8}$ feet wide. They changed the design so the width of the room was $1\frac{3}{4}$ feet shorter than originally planned. Approximately how wide would the new room be with the revised plan?

REVIEW

Write each mixed number as an improper fraction.

26. $5\frac{1}{2}$

27. $3\frac{2}{3}$

28. $7\frac{1}{4}$

List the first five non-zero multiples for each number.

29. 5

30. 7

31. 8

TIC-TAC-TOE ~ INTERVIEW

Interior decorating, engineering, carpet laying, carpentry, architecture, tailoring and plumbing are a few occupations that use fractions regularly. Choose an occupation that uses fractions regularly (it can be one of those above or one approved by your teacher).

Step 1: Write interview questions for someone in that job. Consider what they do on a daily basis and how fractions are used.

Step 2: Interview someone who works in the occupation you chose. Record their responses to your questions.

Step 3: Write a one-page report to inform others about this occupation and how fractions are a necessary aspect of this job. Include the interview questions and the person's responses with your report.

TIC-TAC-TOE ~ ESTIMATION RAP

There are times where estimation is accepted and an exact answer is not needed. However, if you always estimate, problems might arise. For example, if you estimate by rounding to the nearest dollar for something that cost $2.15, you may only bring $2.00 with you. This would not be enough money to buy the item.

Make a list of situations where it is acceptable to estimate. Make another list of times where you should not estimate. Create a rap song using the lists.

ADDING AND SUBTRACTING FRACTIONS

Find sums and differences of fraction expressions.

Sometimes when you add or subtract fractions the denominators are the same. Sometimes you may find that the fractions have different denominators. In this lesson you will learn how to deal with both situations.

EXPLORE!   **PIZZA PARTY!**

Janice was ordering pizzas for her friends. The table shows the fractions of the pizzas each person said they could eat.

	Cheese	Hawaiian	Pepperoni
Janice	$\frac{3}{10}$	$\frac{1}{6}$	$\frac{1}{4}$
Lakelynn	$\frac{1}{5}$	$\frac{1}{3}$	$\frac{3}{8}$
Alvaro	$\frac{3}{5}$	$\frac{1}{2}$	$\frac{5}{8}$
Jory	$\frac{1}{10}$	$\frac{2}{3}$	$\frac{1}{2}$

How much cheese pizza do Lakelynn and Alvaro think they can eat together? Lay out the fraction tiles to represent the amounts of cheese pizza which Lakelynn and Alvaro want. Combine the fraction tiles to find the total. Simplify the fraction, if needed. Draw a picture of the fraction model you used and write the addition equation on paper.

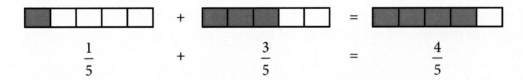

$$\frac{1}{5} \quad + \quad \frac{3}{5} \quad = \quad \frac{4}{5}$$

Step 1: Follow the process shown above to answer the following questions.
      a. How much cheese pizza will Janice and Jory eat together?
      b. How much Hawaiian pizza will Jory and Lakelynn eat together?
      c. How much pepperoni pizza will Lakelynn and Alvaro eat together?

Step 2: Look at the equations. What do you notice about the denominators of the fractions being added and the denominator of the answer? What about the numerators? How might you add fractions with common denominators without using fraction tiles?

How much Hawaiian pizza will Alvaro and Jory eat? Lay out fraction tiles to represent the amount of Hawaiian pizza Alvaro and Jory want.

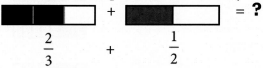 

$$\frac{2}{3} \quad + \quad \frac{1}{2}$$

Find the least common denominator for the two fractions.

2: 2, 4, ⑥, 8

3: 3, ⑥, 9, 12

LCD = 6

Replace the original fraction tiles with equivalent fractions using the LCD. Combine the tiles to find the answer.

$$\frac{4}{6} \quad + \quad \frac{3}{6} \quad = \quad \frac{7}{6}$$

Simplify the fraction, if needed. All improper fractions should be written as mixed numbers.

$$\frac{7}{6} = 1\frac{1}{6}$$

Step 3: Follow the process shown above to answer the following questions. Draw pictures of the fraction tiles used in the process. Write the addition equation on your paper.

a. How much cheese pizza will Janice and Lakelynn eat?

b. How much Hawaiian pizza will Lakelynn and Alvaro eat?

c. How much Hawaiian pizza will Janice and Jory eat?

d. How much pepperoni pizza will Janice and Alvaro eat?

e. How much pepperoni pizza will Janice and Jory eat?

f. How much pepperoni pizza will Alvaro and Jory eat?

Step 4: How might you add fractions with unlike denominators without using fraction tiles?

ADD OR SUBTRACT FRACTIONS WITH COMMON DENOMINATORS

1. Add or subtract the numerators.
2. Write the sum or difference over the common denominator.
3. Simplify the fraction.

ADD OR SUBTRACT FRACTIONS WITH UNLIKE DENOMINATORS

1. Rewrite the fractions using the least common denominator (LCD).
2. Add or subtract the numerators.
3. Write the sum or difference over the common denominator.
4. Simplify the fraction.

After adding, subtracting, multiplying or dividing fractions, you must simplify the fraction. This means writing the fraction in simplest form, then changing improper fractions to mixed numbers if necessary.

EXAMPLE 1

Kiley practiced $\frac{1}{8}$ of her piano music in the morning. That afternoon she practiced $\frac{3}{8}$ of her music. What fraction of her piano music did she practice?

SOLUTION

Write the problem.

$$\frac{1}{8}+\frac{3}{8}$$

Add the numerators and write the sum over the common denominator.

$$\frac{1+3}{8}=\frac{4}{8}$$

Simplify the fraction.

$$\frac{4}{8}=\frac{1}{2}$$

Kiley practiced $\frac{1}{2}$ of her piano music.

EXAMPLE 2

Find the value of $\dfrac{5}{6}-\dfrac{1}{6}$.

SOLUTION

Subtract the numerators. Write the difference over the common denominator.

$$\frac{5-1}{6}=\frac{4}{6}$$

Simplify the fraction.

$$\frac{4}{6}=\frac{2}{3}$$

$$\frac{5}{6}-\frac{1}{6}=\frac{2}{3}$$

EXAMPLE 3

Mallory made $\frac{3}{4}$ gallon of ice cream. Logan made $\frac{1}{2}$ gallon. How many total gallons of ice cream do they have together?

SOLUTION

Write the problem.

$$\frac{3}{4}+\frac{1}{2}$$

Find the least common denominator for the set of fractions.

2: 2, ④, 6
4: ④, 8, 12

Rewrite the fractions using the LCD.

$$\frac{3}{4}=\frac{3}{4} \qquad \frac{1}{2}=\frac{2}{4}$$

Add the numerators.

$$\frac{3}{4}+\frac{2}{4}=\frac{3+2}{4}=\frac{5}{4}$$

Change the improper fraction to a mixed number.

$$\frac{5}{4}=1\frac{1}{4}$$

Mallory and Logan made a total of $1\frac{1}{4}$ gallons of ice cream.

EXAMPLE 4

SOLUTION

Find the value of $\dfrac{2}{3} - \dfrac{1}{4}$.

Find the LCD.

3: 3, 6, 9, ⑫
4: 4, 8, ⑫ 16

Rewrite the fraction using the LCD.

$$\dfrac{2}{3} = \dfrac{8}{12}$$

$$\dfrac{1}{4} = \dfrac{3}{12}$$

Subtract the numerators.

$$\dfrac{8}{12} - \dfrac{3}{12} = \dfrac{8-3}{12} = \dfrac{5}{12}$$

$$\dfrac{2}{3} - \dfrac{1}{4} = \dfrac{5}{12}$$

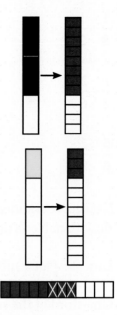

EXERCISES

Find each sum or difference. Write in simplest form.

1. $\dfrac{1}{4} + \dfrac{1}{4}$

2. $\dfrac{3}{5} + \dfrac{1}{5}$

3. $\dfrac{1}{8} + \dfrac{5}{8}$

4. $\dfrac{1}{10} + \dfrac{5}{10}$

5. $\dfrac{7}{9} + \dfrac{5}{9}$

6. $\dfrac{5}{6} - \dfrac{3}{6}$

7. $\dfrac{7}{8} - \dfrac{5}{8}$

8. $\dfrac{9}{15} - \dfrac{4}{15}$

9. $\dfrac{9}{11} - \dfrac{3}{11}$

10. Isaiah surveyed his class to see whether they thought the American beaver was appropriate as the animal symbol for Oregon. Four-eighths of the class thought it was a good choice. Three-eighths of the class thought another animal should be chosen as the Oregon animal symbol. One-eighth of his class did not want to answer the survey. What fraction of his class answered the survey?

11. Jace ran $\frac{3}{10}$ mile on Monday. On Tuesday he ran $\frac{5}{10}$ mile. How much further did he run on Tuesday than Monday?

Find each sum or difference. Write in simplest form.

12. $\dfrac{1}{8} + \dfrac{1}{2}$

13. $\dfrac{5}{12} + \dfrac{4}{6}$

14. $\dfrac{3}{10} + \dfrac{2}{5}$

15. $\dfrac{1}{2} + \dfrac{2}{6}$

16. $\dfrac{3}{4} + \dfrac{2}{3}$

17. $\dfrac{2}{3} - \dfrac{1}{2}$

18. $\dfrac{5}{6} - \dfrac{2}{8}$

19. $\dfrac{5}{9} - \dfrac{1}{3}$

20. $\dfrac{11}{12} - \dfrac{3}{4}$

21. Natasha's desk measured $\frac{3}{4}$ meter wide. Neil's desk was $\frac{2}{3}$ meter wide. How much wider was Natasha's desk than Neil's desk?

22. Lara ate $\frac{1}{2}$ of a sub sandwich. Lucas ate $\frac{3}{4}$ of a sub sandwich. How much did they eat altogether?

23. One-third of the students Ms. Jarrett teaches are sixth graders. Five-twelfths of the students she teaches are seventh graders. The rest are eighth graders.
   a. What fraction of her students are 6th and 7th graders?
   b. What fraction of her students are 8th graders?

24. Aaron rode his bike off a jump $\frac{7}{12}$ yard tall. The next day he rode his bike off a jump $\frac{8}{9}$ yard tall. How much taller was the second jump than the first jump?

REVIEW

Draw a line with the given measure.

25. $2\frac{1}{8}$ in

26. $4\frac{3}{4}$ in

27. $1\frac{1}{2}$ in

Estimate each difference.

28. $\dfrac{9}{10} - \dfrac{3}{8}$

29. $\dfrac{11}{12} - \dfrac{1}{5}$

30. $5\frac{1}{8} - 2\frac{1}{4}$

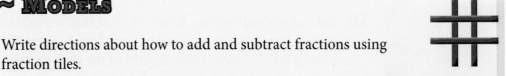

TIC-TAC-TOE ~ MODELS

Write directions about how to add and subtract fractions using fraction tiles.

Have a parent or classmate follow your directions to see if they work. Make any needed changes to your directions so they are clear and useful.

Create a brochure using your directions to teach students how to use fraction tiles to show addition or subtraction of fractions.

ADDING AND SUBTRACTING MIXED NUMBERS

Find sums and differences of expressions that include mixed numbers.

Mixed numbers are used in many real-world situations. Measurements are often given as mixed numbers. Amounts of each ingredient in recipes are also in mixed number form. You will need to add or subtract mixed numbers to solve problems in many situations.

EXPLORE!   **MIXING PAINT**

Kazi painted his bedroom. He mixed different colors of paint together to make new and exciting shades.

Step 1: Kazi purchased two small cans of paint for the ceiling. The can of red paint contained $2\frac{3}{4}$ pints. The can of blue paint contained $1\frac{5}{8}$ pints. He mixed the two cans of paint together. How much paint does he have for the ceiling?

    a. Write the problem as a mathematical expression.
    b. Write each mixed number as an improper fraction.
    c. Rewrite the fractions using the least common denominator.
    d. Find the sum or difference. Simplify your answer and convert it to a mixed number, if needed.

Step 2: Kazi bought $1\frac{1}{6}$ gallons of yellow and $4\frac{1}{3}$ gallons of green paint for the walls. He mixed the two cans of paint together. How much paint does he have available for the walls?

    a. Write the problem as a mathematical expression.
    b. Write each mixed number as an improper fraction.
    c. Rewrite the fractions using the least common denominator.
    d. Find the sum or difference. Simplify your answer and convert it to a mixed number, if needed.

Step 3: Kazi bought $2\frac{1}{5}$ pints of white paint for the trim. When he finished painting he still had $\frac{7}{10}$ pint of white paint left. How much white paint did Kazi use?

    a. Write the problem as a mathematical expression.
    b. Write each mixed number as an improper fraction.
    c. Rewrite the fractions using the least common denominator.
    d. Find the sum or difference. Simplify your answer and convert it to a mixed number, if needed.

Step 4: Explain in your own words how to add or subtract mixed numbers using the method in this Explore!

EXAMPLE 1

Find the value of $3\frac{1}{4} + 1\frac{2}{3}$.

SOLUTION

Change each mixed number to an improper fraction.

$$3\frac{1}{4} = \frac{13}{4}$$
$$1\frac{2}{3} = \frac{5}{3}$$

Write equivalent fractions with the least common denominator, 12.

$$\overset{\times 3}{\frac{13}{4}} = \underset{\times 3}{\frac{39}{12}} \quad \text{and} \quad \overset{\times 4}{\frac{5}{3}} = \underset{\times 4}{\frac{20}{12}}$$

Add the numerators.

$$\frac{39}{12} + \frac{20}{12} = \frac{39 + 20}{12} = \frac{59}{12}$$

Write as a mixed number.

$$\frac{59}{12} = 4\frac{11}{12}$$

$3\frac{1}{4} + 1\frac{2}{3} = 4\frac{11}{12}$

EXAMPLE 2

Seth ran a mile around the track. It took him $6\frac{5}{6}$ minutes to run a mile. His friend, Tremaine, also ran a mile on the track. It took Tremaine $7\frac{1}{3}$ minutes to run the mile. How much faster did Seth run than Tremaine?

SOLUTION

Write the problem.

$$7\frac{1}{3} - 6\frac{5}{6}$$

Write the mixed numbers as improper fractions.

$$7\frac{1}{3} = \frac{22}{3}$$
$$6\frac{5}{6} = \frac{41}{6}$$

Write equivalent fractions with the LCD of 6.

$$\frac{22}{3} = \frac{44}{6}$$

Subtract the numerators.

$$\frac{44}{6} - \frac{41}{6} = \frac{44 - 41}{6} = \frac{3}{6}$$

Write the fraction in simplest form.

$$\frac{3}{6} = \frac{1}{2}$$

Seth ran the mile $\frac{1}{2}$ minute faster than Tremaine.

EXERCISES

Find each sum. Write in simplest form.

1. $5\frac{1}{2}+3\frac{1}{2}$

2. $4\frac{2}{3}+1\frac{1}{6}$

3. $1\frac{1}{4}+2\frac{1}{2}$

4. $4\frac{2}{9}+2\frac{2}{3}$

5. $3\frac{2}{5}+2\frac{3}{10}$

6. $1\frac{1}{5}+4\frac{2}{3}$

7. $3\frac{1}{6}+2\frac{3}{4}$

8. $6\frac{4}{9}+4\frac{1}{4}$

9. $3\frac{1}{3}+1\frac{1}{4}$

10. Silas went to the grocery store with his parents. They bought two pounds of carrots. One pound is about $2\frac{1}{5}$ kilograms. Silas wanted to find the number of kilograms in two pounds so he added $2\frac{1}{5}+2\frac{1}{5}$. How many kilograms are equal to two pounds of carrots?

11. Cory nailed two boards together. The first one was $1\frac{5}{6}$ inches thick. The second one was $3\frac{1}{2}$ inches thick. How thick were the two boards together?

12. Natalie poured $7\frac{3}{8}$ ounces of club soda in a glass. She added $2\frac{1}{4}$ ounces of raspberry flavoring to the club soda. How much liquid was in the glass?

Find each difference. Write in simplest form.

13. $3\frac{7}{8}-2\frac{3}{8}$

14. $2\frac{1}{6}-1\frac{1}{3}$

15. $3\frac{3}{4}-\frac{1}{4}$

16. $4\frac{3}{7}-1\frac{3}{14}$

17. $2\frac{4}{5}-1\frac{1}{15}$

18. $8\frac{3}{4}-4\frac{11}{12}$

19. $5\frac{5}{6}-3\frac{1}{5}$

20. $4\frac{1}{5}-2\frac{1}{6}$

21. $9\frac{5}{12}-8\frac{3}{4}$

22. Nate made $6\frac{2}{3}$ quarts of salsa last year. This year he made $10\frac{5}{6}$ quarts of salsa. How much more salsa did he make this year?

23. Consuela spent $2\frac{1}{2}$ hours babysitting for her neighbor on Saturday. The next week she babysat for $3\frac{1}{4}$ hours. How much longer did she babysit the second week?

24. Sari stood $5\frac{1}{3}$ ft tall. Her mom stood $4\frac{5}{6}$ ft tall. How much taller was Sari than her mom?

25. The Asian elephants at the Oregon Zoo weigh different amounts. Packy weighs $6\frac{5}{8}$ tons. His son, Rama, weighs $3\frac{17}{40}$ tons. How much more does Packy weigh than Rama?

Find each sum or difference. Write in simplest form.

26. $\dfrac{1}{2} + \dfrac{3}{8}$

27. $\dfrac{3}{4} + \dfrac{1}{5}$

28. $\dfrac{5}{6} + \dfrac{3}{5}$

29. $\dfrac{9}{10} - \dfrac{3}{5}$

30. $\dfrac{2}{3} - \dfrac{1}{4}$

31. $\dfrac{11}{12} - \dfrac{1}{5}$

TIC-TAC-TOE ~ YOU ARE THE AUTHOR

There are many children's books which include fractions, such as:

The Wishing Club: A Story about Fractions by Donna Jo Napoli
Give Me Half! by Stuart J. Murphy
Fraction Fun by David A. Adler & Nancy Tobin
Working With Fractions by David A. Adler & Edward Miller
Fraction Action by Loreen Leedy
Hershey's Fractions by Jerry Pallotta & Robert C. Bolster
Apple Fractions by Jerry Pallotta & Rob Bolster

Step 1: Read at least two of the books cited.

Step 2: Create a children's book which includes the concept of fractions. The story should be appropriate for children. Create a cover and illustrations for your story.

TIC-TAC-TOE ~ LIGHTS, CAMERA, ACTION

Adding and subtracting fractions occurs everyday.

Step 1: Make of list of situations where adding or subtracting fractions are used. Include problems that can be solved using addition or subtraction of fractions.

Step 2: Write a skit with two or more characters. The plot should have a problem and a solution using addition or subtraction of fractions.

Script Example: Reid: *write what he says.*
Kellene: *write what she says.*
Include any actions they are to take in parentheses, like (walk across stage) or (face each other).

TIC-TAC-TOE ~ TRIATHLON

A triathlon is an endurance event that consists of swimming, cycling and running. The length of each segment varies depending on the triathlon. In 2008 there were many triathlons around the state of Oregon. Answer the questions below about participants in different triathlons.

1. Pacific Crest Olympic Triathlon – Sunriver, Oregon

   Swim: $\frac{15}{16}$ miles   *Cycle: 28 miles*   *Run: $6\frac{1}{5}$ miles*

   a. How long is the entire triathlon?

   b. Marita has $2\frac{1}{8}$ miles left in the running segment. How far has she traveled so far?

2. Lincoln City Sprint Triathlon – Lincoln City, Oregon

   Swim: $\frac{15}{32}$ mile   *Cycle: $9\frac{3}{5}$ miles*   *Run: $3\frac{1}{10}$ miles*

   a. How long is the entire triathlon?

   b. Quan has finished the swimming segment and has biked 6 miles. How far does he still need to go to finish the triathlon?

3. Granite Man Triathlon – Jacksonville, Oregon

   Swim: $\frac{3}{5}$ mile   *Cycle: 13 miles*   *Run: $3\frac{1}{10}$ miles*

   a. How long is the entire triathlon?

   b. Jerome has $2\frac{1}{8}$ miles left in the cycling segment. How many miles is he from the finish line?

4. Solstice Triathlon – La Grande, Oregon

   Swim: $\frac{3}{5}$ mile   *Cycle: $15\frac{1}{2}$ miles*   *Run: $6\frac{1}{5}$ miles*

   a. How long is the entire triathlon?

   b. LeAnne has $1\frac{1}{4}$ miles left in the cycling segment. How far has she traveled from the starting line of the triathlon?

5. Canby Telcoms Gator Grinder Triathlon – Canby, Oregon

   Swim: $\frac{25}{88}$ mile   *Cycle: 12 miles*   *Run: $3\frac{1}{10}$ miles*

   a. How long is the entire triathlon?

   b. Carlos has almost finished the swimming segment. He had completed $\frac{21}{88}$ mile so far. How far does he still need to go to finish the swimming segment?

   c. How far does Carlos need to go to finish the triathlon?

ADDING AND SUBTRACTING BY RENAMING

 Calculate sums and differences of mixed numbers by renaming.

Y ou learned one method for adding and subtracting mixed numbers in **Lesson 10**. You converted each mixed number into an improper fraction and followed the process for adding or subtracting two fractions. Another method for adding or subtracting mixed numbers is called renaming. Renaming can also be called borrowing or regrouping.

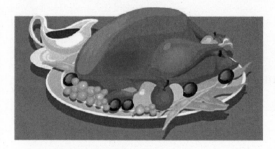

Paula bought a turkey for a family dinner. It weighed $10\frac{3}{4}$ pounds. Her mother did not realize Paula had bought a turkey. Her mother also bought a turkey that weighed $12\frac{2}{3}$ pounds. How many total pounds of turkey did they have for the family dinner?

Write the problem.

$$10\frac{3}{4} + 12\frac{2}{3}$$

Rewrite the fractions using the LCD, 12.

$$10\frac{9}{12} + 12\frac{8}{12}$$

Add each part of the mixed numbers.

$$\begin{array}{r} 10\frac{9}{12} \\ + 12\frac{8}{12} \\ \hline 22\frac{17}{12} \end{array}$$

Rename the improper fraction as a mixed number.

$$\frac{17}{12} = 1\frac{5}{12}$$

Add the sum of the whole numbers to the renamed fraction.

$$22 + 1\frac{5}{12} = 23\frac{5}{12}$$

Paula's family had a total of $23\frac{5}{12}$ pounds of turkey for dinner.

How much larger was the turkey Paula's mother bought than the one Paula had purchased?

Write the problem.

$$12\frac{2}{3} - 10\frac{3}{4}$$

Rewrite the fractions using the LCD, 12.

$$12\frac{8}{12} - 10\frac{9}{12}$$

> If the second fraction is larger than the first fraction, you must rename the first fraction. Borrow 1 from 12 and rename as $\frac{12}{12}$.

Rename $12\frac{8}{12}$ as $11\frac{12}{12} + \frac{8}{12}$ which is $11\frac{20}{12}$.

$$\begin{array}{r} 11\frac{20}{12} \\ - 10\frac{9}{12} \\ \hline 1\frac{11}{12} \end{array}$$

Subtract each part of the mixed numbers.

The turkey Paula's mother bought was $1\frac{11}{12}$ pounds larger than Paula's turkey.

ADDING AND SUBTRACTING BY RENAMING

1. Rewrite the fractions using the LCD.
2. Rename before subtracting, if necessary.
3. Add or subtract the fractions.
4. Add or subtract the whole numbers.
5. Rename after adding, if necessary.

There are two situations where renaming mixed numbers to find the sum or difference is needed.

- ◆ Rename when subtracting if the fraction in the first number is smaller than the fraction in the second number.
- ◆ Rename when adding if the two fractions add to more than 1.

EXAMPLE 1

Find the value of $4\frac{3}{5} + 2\frac{7}{10}$.

SOLUTION

Rewrite the fractions using the LCD, 10.

$$4\frac{6}{10} + 2\frac{7}{10}$$

Add the fractions and the whole numbers.

$$\begin{array}{r} 4\frac{6}{10} \\ + 2\frac{7}{10} \\ \hline 6\frac{13}{10} \end{array}$$

Rename the improper fraction.

$$6\frac{13}{10} = 6 + 1\frac{3}{10} = 7\frac{3}{10}$$

$$4\frac{3}{5} + 2\frac{7}{10} = 7\frac{3}{10}$$

EXAMPLE 2

Mahavir biked $14\frac{5}{6}$ miles on Saturday. He biked $18\frac{1}{4}$ miles on Sunday. How much further did he bike on Sunday?

SOLUTION

Write the problem.

$$18\frac{1}{4} - 14\frac{5}{6}$$

Rewrite using the LCD, 12.

$$18\frac{3}{12} - 14\frac{10}{12}$$

Rename the first fraction because $\frac{3}{12}$ is smaller than $\frac{10}{12}$.

$$\begin{array}{r} 17\frac{15}{12} \\ - 14\frac{10}{12} \\ \hline 3\frac{5}{12} \end{array}$$

Rename $18\frac{3}{12}$ as $17\frac{15}{12}$.

Mahavir rode $3\frac{5}{12}$ miles further on Sunday.

EXAMPLE 3

The longest python on record was 33 feet long. The average male python grows to be $18\frac{1}{6}$ feet long. What is the difference between the average male python and the world's longest python?

SOLUTION

Write the problem. $33 - 18\frac{1}{6}$

Rename 33 as $32\frac{6}{6}$.

$$\begin{array}{r} 32\frac{6}{6} \\ - 18\frac{1}{6} \\ \hline 14\frac{5}{6} \end{array}$$

The world's longest python was $14\frac{5}{6}$ feet longer than the average male python.

EXERCISES

1. Explain one type of problem when renaming should be used to add or subtract mixed numbers.

2. Copy and complete each set of equivalent mixed numbers.

    a. $4\frac{1}{4} = \underline{}\frac{5}{4}$ **b.** $2\frac{2}{5} = 1\frac{}{5}$ **c.** $6\frac{7}{4} = \underline{}\frac{3}{4}$

Find each sum or difference. Write in simplest form.

3. $2\frac{3}{5} + 4\frac{4}{5}$ **4.** $6\frac{2}{3} + 5\frac{5}{6}$ **5.** $9\frac{7}{8} - 1\frac{3}{8}$

6. $10\frac{3}{7} - 7\frac{5}{7}$ **7.** $8\frac{1}{2} + 3\frac{3}{4}$ **8.** $15\frac{1}{3} - 10\frac{1}{6}$

9. $3 - 1\frac{3}{10}$ **10.** $4\frac{11}{12} + 1\frac{1}{3}$ **11.** $8\frac{2}{3} - 7\frac{5}{6}$

12. $22\frac{1}{2} + 10\frac{5}{7}$ **13.** $7 - 3\frac{5}{8}$ **14.** $6\frac{3}{5} - 1\frac{1}{6}$

15. A junior-sized football is $10\frac{3}{8}$ inches long and $5\frac{7}{8}$ inches wide. What is the difference between the football's length and width?

16. Kirk caught a fish that weighed $2\frac{9}{16}$ pounds. His little brother caught a fish that weighed $3\frac{3}{4}$ pounds. What was the total weight of the fish the boys caught?

17. Owen walked $1\frac{4}{5}$ miles on Tuesday and $3\frac{1}{2}$ miles on Wednesday. How far did he walk in the two days combined?

18. A bag contained 2 cups of raisins. Five-eighths of a cup of raisins was used in recipe. How many cups of raisins remain in the bag?

19. Alberto and Marco wrote songs for their band. Alberto's song was $2\frac{1}{2}$ minutes long. Marco's song was $4\frac{1}{6}$ minutes long. How much longer was Marco's song than Alberto's song?

20. How do you know when you need to rename one of the numbers when subtracting mixed numbers?

21. The rim on a basketball hoop is 10 feet off the ground. Ron jumped and reached $8\frac{5}{8}$ feet off the ground. How much higher would Ron need to jump to touch the rim?

REVIEW

Write two equivalent fractions for each fraction.

22. $\dfrac{6}{8}$ **23.** $\dfrac{1}{3}$ **24.** $\dfrac{10}{10}$

Find each sum or difference. Write in simplest form.

25. $\dfrac{4}{9} - \dfrac{1}{3}$ **26.** $\dfrac{1}{5} + \dfrac{9}{10}$ **27.** $\dfrac{3}{4} - \dfrac{1}{6}$

28. $\dfrac{7}{10} - \dfrac{3}{20}$ **29.** $\dfrac{1}{8} + \dfrac{1}{3}$ **30.** $\dfrac{5}{21} + \dfrac{6}{7}$

Tic-Tac-Toe ~ Create the Problem

Instead of finding the sum of an addition problem, you must find two addends that equal a given sum.

Write two addition problems that equal the given sum. At least one problem in each set must have two addends with unlike denominators.

Example: $? + ? = \dfrac{1}{2}$

$\dfrac{1}{8} + \dfrac{3}{8} = \dfrac{4}{8} = \dfrac{1}{2}$ OR $\dfrac{1}{3} + \dfrac{1}{6} = \dfrac{2}{6} + \dfrac{1}{6} = \dfrac{3}{6} = \dfrac{1}{2}$

The sums are:

1. $\dfrac{1}{4}$ **2.** $\dfrac{1}{3}$ **3.** $\dfrac{3}{7}$ **4.** $\dfrac{5}{18}$ **5.** $\dfrac{3}{4}$ **6.** $\dfrac{7}{8}$

7. $\dfrac{11}{14}$ **8.** $\dfrac{6}{13}$ **9.** $\dfrac{7}{15}$ **10.** $\dfrac{5}{6}$ **11.** $\dfrac{7}{12}$ **12.** $\dfrac{2}{5}$

PERIMETER WITH FRACTIONS

LESSON 12

🎯 Add lengths, including fractions and mixed numbers, of the sides of polygons to find perimeters.

If you walk around a football field or a city block, you have traveled the perimeter of something. **Perimeter** is the distance around a closed figure. When you walk all the way around a football field, you have walked its perimeter. When you travel down each side of a city block and back to your starting point, you have traveled the perimeter of the block.

A **polygon** is a closed figure formed by three or more line segments. To find the perimeter of any given polygon you add the lengths of all sides.

```
┌─────────────────────────────────────┐
│         FINDING PERIMETER            │
│                                      │
│  1. Measure all sides (if necessary).│
│  2. Add the lengths of all sides     │
│     together.                        │
└─────────────────────────────────────┘
```

EXAMPLE 1   **Measure each side of the rectangle. Find the perimeter of the rectangle.**

SOLUTION   Use a ruler to measure each side of the shape to the nearest sixteenth of an inch.

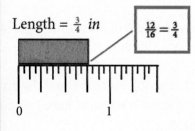   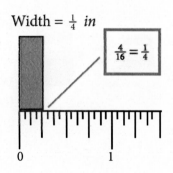

Length = $\frac{3}{4}$ in $\boxed{\frac{12}{16} = \frac{3}{4}}$ Width = $\frac{1}{4}$ in $\boxed{\frac{4}{16} = \frac{1}{4}}$

Add all four sides of the rectangle together. $\frac{3}{4} + \frac{1}{4} + \frac{3}{4} + \frac{1}{4} = \frac{8}{4}$

Simplify. $\frac{8}{4} = 2$ ┌──────────────────────┐
                                    │ **Opposite sides of**   │
                                    │ **rectangles are the same** │
                                    │ **length.**   │
                                    └──────────────────────┘

The perimeter of the rectangle is 2 inches.

EXAMPLE 2

Use the given measurements to find the perimeter of the polygon.

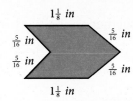

SOLUTION

Add the lengths of all sides together.

$1\frac{1}{8} + \frac{5}{16} + \frac{5}{16} + 1\frac{1}{8} + \frac{5}{16} + \frac{5}{16}$

Change the mixed numbers to improper fractions. $1\frac{1}{8} = \frac{9}{8}$

Use the LCD to rename the fractions.

The LCD is 16. $\frac{9}{8} = \frac{18}{16}$

Add the sides of the polygon.

$\frac{18}{16} + \frac{5}{16} + \frac{5}{16} + \frac{18}{16} + \frac{5}{16} + \frac{5}{16} = \frac{56}{16}$

Simplify.

$\frac{56}{16} = \frac{7}{2} = 3\frac{1}{2}$ or $\frac{56}{16} = 3\frac{8}{16} = 3\frac{1}{2}$

The perimeter of the polygon is $3\frac{1}{2}$ inches.

EXAMPLE 3

Brayden went for a walk in Portland. He walked in a rectangular pattern around a city block. First he walked $66\frac{2}{3}$ yards. He turned right and walked $76\frac{1}{6}$ yards. He turned right two more times and ended up where he started. What was the perimeter of the city block?

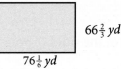

$66\frac{2}{3}$ yd

$76\frac{1}{6}$ yd

SOLUTION

Brayden walked in a rectangular pattern.
Add the four sides.

$66\frac{2}{3} + 76\frac{1}{6} + 66\frac{2}{3} + 76\frac{1}{6} = ?$ yards

Use the LCD to rename the fractions.
The LCD is 6.

$66\frac{2}{3} = 66\frac{4}{6}$

Add the sides of the city block.

$66\frac{4}{6} + 76\frac{1}{6} + 66\frac{4}{6} + 76\frac{1}{6} = 284\frac{10}{6}$ yards

Simplify.

$\frac{10}{6} = 1\frac{4}{6} \rightarrow 284 + 1 + \frac{4}{6} = 285\frac{4}{6} = 285\frac{2}{3}$

The perimeter of the city block Brayden walked was $285\frac{2}{3}$ yards.

EXAMPLE 4

SOLUTION

Use the given measurement to find the perimeter of the square.

Add all four sides of the square together. $1\frac{1}{2} + 1\frac{1}{2} + 1\frac{1}{2} + 1\frac{1}{2} = 4\frac{4}{2}$

Simplify. $4\frac{4}{2} = 4 + 2 = 6$

The perimeter of the square is 6 inches.

$1\frac{1}{2}$ in

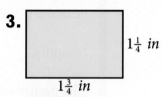

All sides of a square are the same length.

EXERCISES

Use the given measurements to find the perimeter of each rectangle. Write in simplest form.

1. 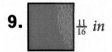 $\frac{1}{8}$ in
$\frac{5}{8}$ in

2. $\frac{13}{16}$ in
$\frac{7}{16}$ in

3. $1\frac{1}{4}$ in
$1\frac{3}{4}$ in

4. 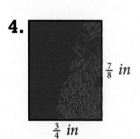 $\frac{7}{8}$ in
$\frac{3}{4}$ in

5. $\frac{1}{2}$ in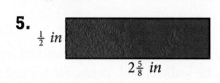
$2\frac{5}{8}$ in

6. $1\frac{9}{16}$ in
$1\frac{1}{8}$ in

7. Measure and record the lengths of the sides of your desk or a table to the nearest quarter inch. Find the perimeter.

8. Measure and record the lengths of the sides of a piece of notebook paper to the nearest sixteenth inch. Find the perimeter.

Use the given measurement to find the perimeter of each square. Write in simplest form.

9. 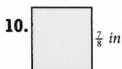 $\frac{11}{16}$ in

10. $\frac{7}{8}$ in

11.  $1\frac{1}{4}$ in

Measure one side of each squares to the nearest sixteenth of an inch using a customary ruler. Find each perimeter. Write in simplest form.

12.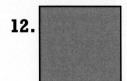

13.

14.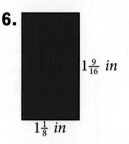

Find the perimeter of each polygon. Write in simplest form.

15.
$\frac{7}{8}$ in, $1\frac{11}{16}$ in, $\frac{7}{8}$ in, $\frac{7}{8}$ in, $1\frac{11}{16}$ in, $\frac{7}{8}$ in

16.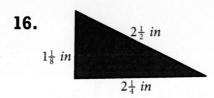
$1\frac{1}{8}$ in, $2\frac{1}{2}$ in, $2\frac{1}{4}$ in

17.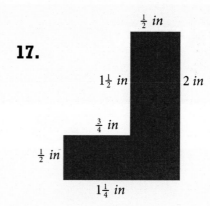
$\frac{1}{2}$ in, $1\frac{1}{2}$ in, 2 in, $\frac{3}{4}$ in, $\frac{1}{2}$ in, $1\frac{1}{4}$ in

18. Jenna's room was a perfect square. The length of one wall measured $15\frac{1}{6}$ feet. What is the perimeter of Jenna's room?

19. Thi walked $20\frac{1}{8}$ yards toward the office. She turned right and walked $35\frac{3}{4}$ yards toward the parking lot. She walked in a rectangle until she was back where she started. What is the perimeter of the area Thi walked?

REVIEW

Find each sum or difference. Write in simplest form.

20. $9\frac{1}{4} - 3\frac{3}{4}$

21. $15\frac{1}{6} - 9\frac{5}{6}$

22. $40\frac{1}{2} - 22\frac{2}{3}$

23. $2\frac{1}{3} + 3\frac{3}{4}$

24. $9\frac{4}{5} + 3\frac{1}{6}$

25. $2\frac{1}{6} + 8\frac{5}{8}$

Simplify each fraction. Write as a mixed number.

26. $\frac{26}{10}$

27. $\frac{84}{9}$

28. $\frac{420}{105}$

Tic-Tac-Toe ~ Measure the Perimeter

Picture frames come in many sizes.

Step 1: Find ten or more different sized frames at home or at a store (they do not all have to be rectangular).

Step 2: Use a customary ruler or measuring tape to measure the lengths of the sides of each frame to the nearest sixteenth of an inch.

Step 3: Draw a sketch of the shape of each frame. Record the lengths of the sides you measured.

Step 4: Calculate the perimeter of each frame.

Vocabulary

perimeter
polygon

 Estimate sums and differences of expressions with fractions and mixed numbers.
Find sums and differences of fraction expressions.
Find sums and differences of expressions that include mixed numbers.
Calculate sums and differences of mixed numbers by renaming.
Add lengths, including fractions and mixed numbers, of the sides of polygons to find perimeters.

Lesson 8 ~ Estimating Sums and Differences

Estimate each sum or difference. Round to 0, $\frac{1}{2}$ or 1 before adding or subtracting.

1. $\frac{1}{8} + \frac{2}{3}$

2. $\frac{4}{10} + \frac{7}{8}$

3. $\frac{8}{9} - \frac{2}{5}$

4. $\frac{4}{7} - \frac{1}{9}$

5. $\frac{9}{10} + \frac{1}{6}$

6. $\frac{11}{20} - \frac{8}{15}$

Estimate each sum or difference. Round to the nearest whole number before adding or subtracting.

7. $1\frac{7}{8} + 2\frac{8}{9}$

8. $6\frac{3}{5} + 2\frac{1}{8}$

9. $3\frac{2}{3} - 1\frac{6}{7}$

10. $4\frac{5}{13} - 2\frac{1}{6}$

11. $10\frac{1}{5} + 4\frac{1}{9}$

12. $12\frac{4}{5} - 1\frac{1}{6}$

Lesson 9 ~ Adding and Subtracting Fractions

Find each sum or difference. Write in simplest form.

13. $\frac{3}{8} + \frac{2}{8}$

14. $\frac{6}{7} + \frac{6}{7}$

15. $\frac{8}{9} - \frac{2}{9}$

16. $\frac{5}{6} - \frac{1}{6}$

17. $\frac{7}{10} + \frac{5}{6}$

18. $\frac{4}{5} + \frac{7}{8}$

19. $\dfrac{7}{9} - \dfrac{4}{15}$

20. $\dfrac{11}{12} - \dfrac{1}{5}$

21. $\dfrac{1}{9} + \dfrac{3}{4}$

22. Corrie had $\frac{1}{2}$ cup of brown sugar. She borrowed $\frac{1}{4}$ cup of brown sugar in order to have enough for her chocolate chip cookie recipe. How much brown sugar did the recipe call for?

23. Tonda's sunflower plant was $\frac{7}{8}$ yard tall. Jasmine's sunflower plant was $\frac{2}{3}$ yard tall. How much taller was Tonda's sunflower plant than Jasmine's sunflower plant?

Lesson 10 ~ Adding and Subtracting Mixed Numbers

Find each sum or difference. Write in simplest form.

24. $1\frac{1}{5} + 2\frac{4}{5}$

25. $2\frac{3}{4} + 1\frac{1}{2}$

26. $3\frac{5}{8} - 1\frac{1}{8}$

27. $5\frac{14}{16} - 2\frac{5}{8}$

28. $5\frac{1}{9} + 2\frac{3}{4}$

29. $4\frac{6}{7} + 2\frac{2}{3}$

30. $2\frac{3}{5} - 1\frac{3}{4}$

31. $5\frac{1}{2} - 3\frac{5}{9}$

32. $4\frac{2}{3} - 1\frac{1}{7}$

33. Travis used $4\frac{3}{4}$ quarts of oil when he changed his car's oil. A week later he checked his oil. He had to put $1\frac{1}{3}$ quarts of oil in the car because there was a leak. How much oil did Travis use in all?

34. Quinn's dad is $6\frac{1}{2}$ feet tall. Quinn is $5\frac{1}{4}$ feet tall. How much taller is Quinn's dad than Quinn?

Lesson 11 ~ Adding and Subtracting by Renaming

Find each sum or difference using renaming. Write in simplest form.

35. $3\frac{2}{7} + 1\frac{6}{7}$

36. $10 - 4\frac{8}{9}$

37. $13\frac{2}{5} - 9\frac{1}{2}$

38. $7\frac{5}{6} + 3\frac{3}{4}$

39. $5 - 3\frac{1}{3}$

40. $2\frac{4}{5} + 1\frac{7}{10}$

41. Rory made $8\frac{1}{2}$ quarts of punch for a birthday party. Rory had to make $2\frac{5}{8}$ more quarts. How much punch did Rory make altogether?

42. Thurston bought 50 pounds of grain for his cows. At the end of the week he had $7\frac{7}{8}$ pounds of grain left. How many pounds of grain did the cows eat?

Use the given measurements to find the perimeter of each polygon. Write in simplest form.

43.

 SQUARE $2\frac{3}{4}$ in

44.

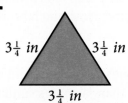 $3\frac{1}{4}$ in $3\frac{1}{4}$ in

$3\frac{1}{4}$ in

45.

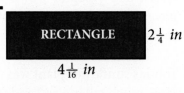 RECTANGLE $2\frac{1}{4}$ in

$4\frac{1}{16}$ in

Use a customary ruler to measure one side of each square to the nearest sixteenth of an inch. Find each perimeter. Write in simplest form.

46.

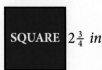

47.

48.

49. Omid ran around the perimeter of a basketball court. The width of the court was $50\frac{1}{4}$ ft and the length was $90\frac{1}{2}$ ft . He ended where he began. What is the distance that Omid ran?

TIC-TAC-TOE ~ FIND THE SUM

$$\frac{1}{2} + \frac{1}{3} + \frac{1}{4}$$

There are times where you will be finding the sum of more than two fractions or mixed numbers. You will have to change all mixed numbers to improper fractions to add the multiple fractions. Then find the least common denominator (LCD) of the entire set of fractions.

Example: $1\frac{1}{2} + \frac{1}{4} + \frac{3}{8}$

Rewrite $1\frac{1}{2}$ as $\frac{3}{2}$

The LCD of $\frac{3}{2}$, $\frac{1}{4}$ and $\frac{3}{8}$ is 8.

Use the LCD for the set of fractions. Rewrite each fraction.

$\frac{3}{2} = \frac{12}{8}$, $\frac{1}{4} = \frac{2}{8}$, $\frac{3}{8}$ remains $\frac{3}{8}$

Add the numerators over the common denominator.

$\frac{12}{8} + \frac{2}{8} + \frac{3}{8} = \frac{12+2+3}{8} = \frac{17}{8}$

Simplify. Write improper fractions as mixed numbers.

$\frac{17}{8} = 2\frac{1}{8}$

Write 20 different simplified fractions or mixed numbers on 3×5 cards. Draw three cards from the stack and write an addition equation using the three fractions. Use the process above to find the sum. Do this for at least ten problems.

CAREER FOCUS

MICK
FIREFIGHTER/PARAMEDIC
PORTLAND, OREGON

I am a firefighter and paramedic. I work a 24-hour shift, and then have 48 hours off. I respond to emergencies at any time of the day or night. I may be called to fires in houses or buildings. I might also be called for a medical emergency, car accident or any other situation where people need help. A typical day at the fire station includes training or practicing drills related to firefighting. Firefighters also shop and cook for themselves. I help make sure all of our equipment is clean and in good working condition. Most importantly, I need to be prepared for an emergency at all times.

I use math whenever I fight a fire. I have to figure out how much pressure is needed in the hoses to ensure water is available everywhere it is needed. I also need to know the pressure of water coming out of a fire hydrant so I can estimate how much water is available. My math must be accurate to ensure that every situation is as safe as possible and that fires are fought most efficiently. I also have to use calculations about water pressures and anchoring on the fireboat.

Sometimes, in medical emergencies, I give people medications. I need to use math to figure out how much the patient weighs before I can give a medication. Estimating how much somebody weighs helps me know how much medicine or fluid to give them. If my estimate is off, it could lead to a dangerous situation for the patient.

Firefighters must go to college for two years. You must go to college for another two years to become a paramedic. After you are hired as a firefighter and paramedic, you have about 9 -12 months of training to complete. A starting firefighter makes about $45,000 per year. An officer makes over $100,000 per year.

The best thing about my job is helping people and putting smiles on their faces. When people call 911, they need help and are glad to see me arrive.

BLOCK 3 ~ FRACTIONS AND DECIMALS
MULTIPLYING AND DIVIDING FRACTIONS

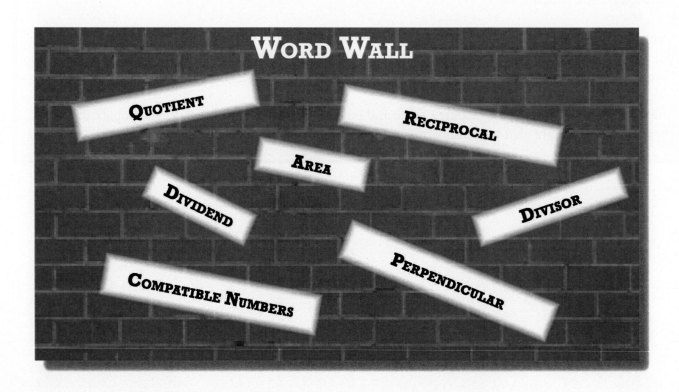

WORD WALL

QUOTIENT

RECIPROCAL

AREA

DIVIDEND

DIVISOR

PERPENDICULAR

COMPATIBLE NUMBERS

BLOCK 3 ~ MULTIPLYING AND DIVIDING FRACTIONS

TIC - TAC - TOE

ADVERTISEMENTS

Find advertisements that state "Buy One, Get One Half Off." Figure out the savings for purchases.

See page 96 for details.

MULTIPLICATION OF MULTIPLE FRACTIONS

Solve multiplication problems with three or more fractions.

See page 76 for details.

DREAM HOUSE

Draw a one story dream house. Find the square footage of the blueprint.

See page 101 for details.

CHANGING RECIPES

Find the amount of each ingredient to cut a recipe in half, make $1\frac{1}{2}$ times or triple it.

See page 96 for details.

FRACTION BINGO

Design a fraction BINGO game.

See page 88 for details.

CELL PHONE PLANS

Create a poster to compare the price-per-person and the minutes-per-person for family cell phone plans.

See page 84 for details.

HOW MANY MINUTES?

Find the number of minutes in a fraction of an hour.

See page 92 for details.

LANDSCAPING

Find the number of edging blocks you would need around each flower bed in a backyard.

See page 101 for details.

TEACH ME!

Create a flap book to teach other students how to multiply and divide fractions using models.

See page 80 for details.

MULTIPLYING FRACTIONS WITH MODELS

Use models to multiply fractions.

EXPLORE!   **FRACTION ACTION**

Find the value of $\frac{1}{6} \times \frac{3}{4}$ (which is read $\frac{1}{6}$ of $\frac{3}{4}$) by completing the following steps.

Step 1: Divide a piece of paper horizontally into as many sections as are shown in the denominator of one of the factors. For $\frac{3}{4}$, divide the paper into 4 horizontal sections.

Step 2: Use blue to color in as many horizontal sections as are shown in the numerator. For $\frac{3}{4}$, color in 3 of the 4 sections.

Step 3: Divide the piece of paper vertically into as many sections as are shown in the denominator of the factor. For $\frac{1}{6}$, divide the paper into 6 vertical sections.

Step 4: Use yellow to color in as many vertical sections as are shown in the numerator. For $\frac{1}{6}$, color in one of the 6 vertical sections.

> Blue and yellow make green.

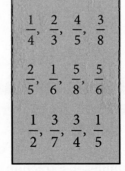

Step 5: The answer to your product is $\frac{\text{number of sections shaded green}}{\text{total number of sections}}$.

$$\frac{1}{6} \times \frac{3}{4} = \frac{3}{24} \quad \rightarrow \quad \frac{3}{24} = \frac{1}{8}$$

> Simplify if necessary.

$$\frac{1}{4}, \frac{2}{3}, \frac{4}{5}, \frac{3}{8}$$

$$\frac{2}{5}, \frac{1}{6}, \frac{5}{8}, \frac{5}{6}$$

$$\frac{1}{2}, \frac{3}{7}, \frac{3}{4}, \frac{1}{5}$$

Step 6: Repeat **Steps 1-5** by finding the product of at least four different pairs of fractions from the purple box.

Step 7: Does it matter which fraction in the equation is shaded first? Explain your reasoning.

EXAMPLE 1

Rafael's mom had $\frac{3}{4}$ cup of blueberries. She split the blueberries among her three children. Each one received $\frac{1}{3}$ of the blueberries. What fraction of a cup of blueberries did each child receive?

SOLUTION

Write the problem.

$$\frac{1}{3} \times \frac{3}{4}$$

Draw a rectangle and divide it into fourths horizontally. Shade $\frac{3}{4}$ of the rectangle, or three of the four sections, with blue.

Divide the rectangle vertically into thirds. Shade $\frac{1}{3}$ of the rectangle, or one of the vertical sections, with yellow.

There are now 12 sections on the rectangle. This is the value of the denominator.

$$\frac{\square}{12}$$

There are 3 sections that were shaded twice. This is the value of the numerator. Simplify.

$$\frac{3}{12} = \frac{1}{4}$$

Each child received $\frac{1}{4}$ cup of blueberries.

EXAMPLE 2

Find the value of $\frac{4}{5} \times \frac{2}{3}$ using models.

SOLUTION

Draw a rectangle and divide it into thirds horizontally. Shade two of the three sections with blue.

Divide the rectangle vertically into fifths. Shade four of the five vertical sections with yellow.

There are 15 sections on the rectangle. This is the value of the denominator.

$$\frac{\square}{15}$$

There are 8 sections shaded twice. This is the value of the numerator.

$$\frac{8}{15}$$

The fraction is in simplest form, so $\frac{4}{5} \times \frac{2}{3} = \frac{8}{15}$.

EXERCISES

1. Find the value of $\frac{3}{8} \times \frac{1}{2}$ by completing the following steps.

    a. Draw a rectangle.

    b. Divide the rectangle horizontally into as many sections as the denominator of the second fraction. Color in as many sections as the numerator of the second fraction.

    c. Divide the square horizontally into as many sections as the denominator of the first fraction. Color in as many sections as the numerator of the first fraction.

    d. Write a fraction where the total number of sections is the denominator and the total number of sections that are colored twice is the numerator.

    e. What is the answer in simplest form?

Use the procedure from Exercise 1 to find each product.

2. $\frac{1}{4} \times \frac{3}{6}$

3. $\frac{5}{6} \times \frac{1}{2}$

4. $\frac{3}{5} \times \frac{1}{3}$

5. $\frac{1}{6} \times \frac{2}{5}$

6. $\frac{2}{4} \times \frac{4}{5}$

7. $\frac{1}{3} \times \frac{4}{6}$

Write the equation to match each of the following models.

8. __ × __ = __

9.  __ × __ = __

10. __ × __ = __

11. A container held $\frac{1}{3}$ cup cream cheese. Becca put $\frac{1}{2}$ of the cream cheese on a bagel. What fraction of a cup of cream cheese did she put on the bagel?

12. About $\frac{7}{10}$ of the earth's surface is water. The Pacific Ocean makes up $\frac{1}{2}$ of this water. What fraction of the earth is covered by the Pacific Ocean?

REVIEW

Find each difference using renaming. Write in simplest form.

13. $4\frac{1}{2} + 2\frac{3}{4}$

14. $1\frac{2}{5} - \frac{3}{4}$

15. $6\frac{1}{6} - 4\frac{2}{3}$

Find each sum. Write in simplest form.

16. $1\frac{1}{2} + 2\frac{1}{6}$

17. $7\frac{1}{4} + 3\frac{4}{7}$

18. $5\frac{1}{3} + 4\frac{1}{4}$

MULTIPLYING FRACTIONS

 Find products of expressions involving two fractions.

Olivia's mom gave her $\frac{2}{3}$ of an hour to work on her homework with Tessa before they left for the grocery store. Olivia and Tessa used $\frac{1}{2}$ of that time for math homework. Olivia thought this equaled $\frac{1}{2}$ hour. Tessa said she was wrong. She said it equaled $\frac{1}{3}$ hour. Who was correct?

Olivia and Tessa wrote the problem as a mathematical expression.

$$\frac{1}{2} \text{ of } \frac{2}{3} \rightarrow \frac{1}{2} \times \frac{2}{3}$$

> Remember that the × symbol can be read "of."

> **MULTIPLYING FRACTIONS**
>
> For any numbers a, b, c, and d:
> $$\frac{a}{b} \times \frac{c}{d} = \frac{a \times c}{b \times d}$$

EXAMPLE 1 | Find the value of $\frac{1}{2} \times \frac{2}{3}$.

SOLUTION

Find the products of the numerators and denominators.

Simplify.
$$\frac{1}{2} \times \frac{2}{3} = \frac{1}{3}$$

$$\frac{1}{2} \times \frac{2}{3} = \frac{1 \times 2}{2 \times 3} = \frac{2}{6}$$

$$\frac{2}{6} = \frac{1}{3}$$

When a numerator and denominator of either fraction have a common factor you can simplify before multiplying.

EXAMPLE 2 | Find the value of $\frac{1}{8} \times \frac{4}{7}$.

SOLUTION

Find a common factor of one numerator and one denominator. The GCF of the numerator, 4, and denominator, 8, is 4.

Divide that numerator and denominator by 4. Write the factor above or below each simplified number in the fractions.

Multiply the numerators and denominators.

$$\frac{1}{8} \times \frac{4}{7} = \frac{1}{14}$$

> Using this method means the fraction will not need to be simplified after multiplying.

$$\frac{1}{8} \times \frac{4}{7} = \frac{1 \times \overset{1}{\cancel{4}}}{\underset{2}{\cancel{8}} \times 7}$$

$$\frac{1 \times 1}{7 \times 2} = \frac{1}{14}$$

EXAMPLE 3

Sandeep had $\frac{3}{8}$ cup of yogurt. She put $\frac{4}{9}$ of the yogurt into a smoothie. What fraction of a cup of yogurt did she use in the smoothie?

SOLUTION

Write the problem.

$$\frac{4}{9} \times \frac{3}{8}$$

The GFC of the numerator, 4, and the denominator, 8, is 4.

Divide that numerator and denominator by 4.

$$\frac{4}{9} \times \frac{3}{8} = \frac{\cancel{4}^{1}}{9} \times \frac{3}{\cancel{8}_{2}}$$

Write the new fraction expression. The numerator 3 and the denominator 9 have a GFC of 3. Divide that numerator and denominator by 3.

$$\frac{1}{_{3}\cancel{9}} \times \frac{\cancel{3}^{1}}{2} = \frac{1 \times 1}{3 \times 2}$$

Multiply the numerators and denominators.

$$\frac{1 \times 1}{3 \times 2} = \frac{1}{6}$$

Sandeep put $\frac{1}{6}$ cup of yogurt in her smoothie.

EXERCISES

Find each product. Write your answer in simplest form.

1. $\frac{1}{3} \times \frac{4}{5}$

2. $\frac{3}{4} \times \frac{1}{2}$

3. $\frac{2}{3} \times \frac{1}{5}$

4. $\frac{4}{5} \times \frac{2}{5}$

5. $\frac{1}{4} \times \frac{4}{5}$

6. $\frac{5}{6} \times \frac{3}{5}$

7. $\frac{4}{7} \times \frac{3}{10}$

8. $\frac{3}{4} \times \frac{2}{3}$

9. $\frac{5}{6} \times \frac{7}{10}$

10. A cinnamon roll recipe requires $\frac{5}{8}$ cup of raisins. Beth wanted to make $\frac{1}{2}$ of the recipe of cinnamon rolls. She only needed $\frac{1}{2}$ of the raisins. How many cups of raisins does she need for half of the cinnamon roll recipe?

11. Four cheerleaders had mastered $\frac{1}{2}$ of their dance routine. However, Sadie was behind. She had only mastered $\frac{1}{2}$ of what the other four cheerleaders had mastered. How much of the dance routine had Sadie mastered?

Simplify the numbers in each fraction before multiplying. Find each product.

12. $\dfrac{1}{15} \times \dfrac{5}{6}$

13. $\dfrac{2}{3} \times \dfrac{3}{5}$

14. $\dfrac{4}{5} \times \dfrac{3}{8}$

15. $\dfrac{2}{7} \times \dfrac{3}{4}$

16. $\dfrac{1}{5} \times \dfrac{10}{13}$

17. $\dfrac{3}{4} \times \dfrac{12}{13}$

18. $\dfrac{4}{15} \times \dfrac{3}{8}$

19. $\dfrac{15}{16} \times \dfrac{4}{9}$

20. $\dfrac{6}{7} \times \dfrac{7}{12}$

21. Da-Shawn made $\frac{3}{4}$ of his shots at basketball practice. Trent made $\frac{2}{5}$ of the number of shots Da-Shawn made. What fraction of shots did Trent make?

22. Camden completed $\frac{12}{15}$ of his math homework in thirty minutes. Catira completed $\frac{3}{4}$ of what Camden had completed in the same amount of time. What fraction of math homework had Catira completed in thirty minutes?

23. Raynesha biked for $\frac{3}{4}$ hour yesterday. Today she plans to bike for $\frac{5}{6}$ the amount of time she did yesterday. How long does she plan to bike today?

REVIEW

Find the GCF of each pair of numbers.

24. 32 and 48

25. 20 and 30

26. 44 and 33

Use the given measurements to find the perimeter of each polygon.

27. $1\frac{1}{2}$ in, $2\frac{1}{2}$ in, 2 in

28. SQUARE $\frac{4}{5}$ in

29. RECTANGLE $7\frac{7}{10}$ in, $6\frac{4}{5}$ in

Tic-Tac-Toe ~ Multiplication of Multiple Fractions

Follow the same procedure for multiplying two fractions when multiplying three or more fractions. Change any mixed numbers to improper fractions before multiplying.

Step 1: Multiply the numerators. Multiply the denominators. Simplify the fraction.

$$\textit{Example:} \quad \frac{1}{2} \times \frac{2}{6} \times \frac{3}{4} \qquad\qquad \frac{1}{2} \times \frac{2}{6} \times \frac{3}{4} = \frac{1 \times 1 \times 1}{1 \times 2 \times 4} = \frac{1}{8}$$

OR

Step 2: Simplify before multiplying. Divide one numerator and one denominator by a common factor. Repeat with other numerators and denominators as applicable. Multiply the numerators and denominators.

$$\textit{Example:} \quad \frac{1}{2} \times \frac{2}{6} \times \frac{3}{4} \qquad\qquad \frac{1}{2} \times \frac{2}{6} \times \frac{3}{4} = \frac{1 \times 2 \times 3}{1 \times 2 \times 4} = \frac{1}{8}$$

Write twenty different fractions or mixed numbers on sticky notes or small pieces of paper. Select three or more fractions and write a multiplication problem with these fractions. Find the product. Repeat ten times using different combinations of fractions. Challenge yourself to select a set of four fractions at least twice.

DIVIDING FRACTIONS WITH MODELS

 Use models to divide fractions.

A group of students wanted to play a game of football in an open field. They marked off 100 yards for the entire football field. They needed to know how many 10 yard sections the 100 yard field covered. This can be written in three different ways.

$$10\overline{)100} \quad \text{or} \quad \frac{100}{10} \quad \text{or} \quad 100 \div 10$$

The students divided the 100 yards into 10 yard sections. It looked something like this diagram.

The students saw that 100 yards divided by 10 yards gave them 10 sections of 10 yards each.

$$\text{divisor} \rightarrow 10\overline{)100} \begin{matrix} \leftarrow \text{quotient} \\ \leftarrow \text{dividend} \end{matrix} \qquad \frac{100}{10} = 10 \begin{matrix} \leftarrow \text{dividend} \\ \leftarrow \text{quotient} \\ \leftarrow \text{divisor} \end{matrix} \qquad 100 \div 10 = 10 \begin{matrix} \leftarrow \text{dividend} \\ \leftarrow \text{quotient} \\ \leftarrow \text{divisor} \end{matrix}$$

In each problem, 100 is the **dividend**, the number being divided. The **divisor** is 10, the number used to divide. The answer to the problem is called the **quotient**.

Dividing requires you to find how many groups of one number fit into another number. The same approach applies when dividing fractions.

EXAMPLE 1	**Maelynn needs to measure $\frac{3}{4}$ cup of milk, but only has a $\frac{1}{4}$ cup measuring cup. How many times will she need to fill it?**
SOLUTION	Write the problem. $\qquad\qquad\qquad\qquad \frac{3}{4} \div \frac{1}{4}$

How many times does $\frac{1}{4}$ fit into $\frac{3}{4}$?

Draw a picture that represents the dividend, $\frac{3}{4}$.

Circle sets that are the size of the divisor, $\frac{1}{4}$.

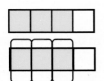

$$\frac{1}{4} \quad \frac{1}{4} \quad \frac{1}{4}$$

Count how many sets of the divisor fit in the dividend to find the quotient. There are 3 circled sets of $\frac{1}{4}$ in $\frac{3}{4}$.

$$\frac{3}{4} \div \frac{1}{4} = 3$$

Maelynn will need to fill the $\frac{1}{4}$ cup measuring cup 3 times.

Example 1 shows how to find the quotient of two fractions with the same denominator. What happens if the fractions have unlike denominators? It is necessary, in this case, to rename the fractions so they have common denominators.

EXAMPLE 2

Clint needs to make a platform that is $\frac{3}{4}$ inch thick. He has boards that are each $\frac{3}{8}$ of an inch thick. How many boards does he need to make the platform?

SOLUTION

Write the problem.

$$\frac{3}{4} \div \frac{3}{8}$$

How many times does $\frac{3}{8}$ fit into $\frac{3}{4}$?

Rename one or both of the fractions so they have common denominators.

$$\frac{3}{4} = \frac{6}{8}$$

Draw a picture that represents the dividend, $\frac{3}{4}$ or $\frac{6}{8}$.

Circle sets that are the size of the divisor, $\frac{3}{8}$.

Count how many sets of the divisor fit in the dividend to find the quotient.

There are 2 circled sets of $\frac{3}{8}$ in $\frac{6}{8}$ or $\frac{3}{4}$.

$$\frac{3}{4} \div \frac{3}{8} = 2$$

Clint will need two boards, each $\frac{3}{8}$ inch thick, to make a $\frac{3}{4}$ inch thick platform.

EXPLORE!   **WHAT FITS?**

Step 1: Choose one expression from the yellow box. (This example uses $\frac{1}{2} \div \frac{1}{8}$.)

Dividend / Divisor

Step 2: If the two fractions in this expression have the same denominator, go to **Step 3.**
If the two fractions have unlike denominators, find a common denominator.

$$\frac{1}{2} = \frac{4}{8}$$

Step 3: Draw a rectangle. Divide it into as many sections as the denominator of the dividend. If you renamed the dividend in **Step 2,** use the new fraction.

Step 4: Color in as many sections as the numerator of the dividend.

Step 5: Circle sets of your divisor in your drawing.

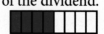

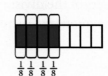

$$\frac{1}{2} \div \frac{1}{4}, \quad \frac{1}{2} \div \frac{1}{8}, \quad \frac{2}{3} \div \frac{1}{6}$$

$$\frac{2}{3} \div \frac{2}{6}, \quad \frac{1}{4} \div \frac{1}{8}, \quad \frac{5}{8} \div \frac{1}{8}$$

$$\frac{3}{4} \div \frac{1}{8}, \quad \frac{1}{3} \div \frac{1}{6}, \quad \frac{2}{3} \div \frac{1}{3}$$

Step 6: Count how many sets of the divisor are circled in your drawing.

Step 7: Write your drawing as an equation with an answer. $\frac{1}{2} \div \frac{1}{8} = 4$ — Quotient

Step 8: Use **Steps 1-7** to find the quotient of at least four different expressions from the yellow box.

EXERCISES

1. $\frac{6}{8} \div \frac{1}{4}$

    a. Rename one or both of the fractions so they have common denominators.
    b. Draw a rectangular model to represent the dividend.
    c. Circle sets in the rectangle that are the size of the divisor.
    d. How many sets of the divisor fit in the dividend? This is the quotient.

Use the procedure from Exercise 1 to find each quotient.

2. $\frac{4}{6} \div \frac{1}{6}$
                   3. $\frac{4}{7} \div \frac{2}{7}$
                   4. $\frac{9}{10} \div \frac{1}{10}$

5. $\frac{6}{10} \div \frac{1}{5}$
                   6. $\frac{6}{9} \div \frac{1}{3}$
                   7. $\frac{8}{12} \div \frac{2}{6}$

Write the equation to match each of the following models.

8. ___ ÷ ___ = ___
                   9. 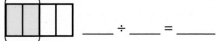 ___ ÷ ___ = ___

10.  ___ ÷ ___ = ___
                   11.  ___ ÷ ___ = ___

12. ___ ÷ ___ = ___
                   13. 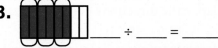 ___ ÷ ___ = ___

14. Treva had a bottle that held $\frac{9}{16}$ ounces of liquid. She had a $\frac{3}{16}$ ounce measuring cup. How many measuring cups of liquid would she need to fill her bottle?

15. Taj took a MAX train through Portland for $\frac{8}{9}$ mile. The MAX train stopped every $\frac{2}{9}$ mile. How many times did the train stop while Taj was on it?

16. Jarrod built a tower of blocks that was $\frac{2}{3}$ meter tall. The blocks were each $\frac{1}{15}$ meter tall. How many blocks did he use?

17. Abir's mom sliced an orange for her. She gave Abir $\frac{2}{3}$ of the orange. Each slice was $\frac{1}{12}$ of the orange. How many slices of orange did Abir have?

REVIEW

Find each product. Write your answer in simplest form.

18. $\frac{1}{3} \times \frac{1}{2}$

19. $\frac{3}{5} \times \frac{5}{8}$

20. $\frac{2}{7} \times \frac{7}{8}$

Find the LCM of each set of numbers.

21. 4, 5

22. 3, 4, 6

23. 3, 5, 6

Find each difference using renaming.

24. $4\frac{3}{4} - 2\frac{7}{8}$

25. $5\frac{1}{8} - 3\frac{1}{3}$

26. $6\frac{3}{5} - 2\frac{11}{15}$

Tic-Tac-Toe ~ Teach Me!

Make a flap book by folding a long sheet of paper lengthwise. Cut just to the fold to create two flaps (as shown in the diagram).

Label one flap "Multiplying Fractions Using Models."
Label the other flap "Dividing Fractions Using Models."

Under the first flap, write directions to teach a classmate how to multiply fractions using models.

Under the second flap, write directions to teach a classmate how to divide fractions using models.

Have a parent or classmate try your directions to see if they work. Make changes to your directions so they are clear and useful, if needed.

DIVIDING FRACTIONS

 Find quotients of expressions involving two fractions.

Drawing a model to find how many of one fraction fits into another fraction helps visualize the quotient. However, it becomes more difficult when the fractions do not divide evenly into each other.

For example: $\dfrac{1}{2} \div \dfrac{3}{8}$

If you were to draw this as in **Lesson 15**, your drawing would show that $\frac{3}{8}$ does not divide evenly into $\frac{1}{2}$.

Reciprocals are used to divide fractions without models. Two numbers are reciprocals if their product is 1. To find the reciprocal of a fraction, "flip" the fraction. The numerator becomes the denominator and the denominator becomes the numerator.

$$\frac{3}{5} \xrightarrow{\text{Reciprocal}} \frac{5}{3} \qquad\qquad \frac{1}{4} \xrightarrow{\text{Reciprocal}} \frac{4}{1}$$

$$\boxed{\checkmark}\ \frac{3}{5} \times \frac{5}{3} = \frac{15}{15} = 1 \qquad\qquad \boxed{\checkmark}\ \frac{1}{4} \times \frac{4}{1} = \frac{4}{4} = 1$$

EXAMPLE 1	**Find the reciprocals of the following numbers.**

a. $\dfrac{2}{3}$ **b.** $\dfrac{1}{7}$ **c.** $\dfrac{5}{6}$

SOLUTIONS

a. Since $\dfrac{2}{3} \times \dfrac{3}{2} = \dfrac{6}{6} = 1$ the reciprocal of $\dfrac{2}{3}$ is $\dfrac{3}{2}$.

b. Since $\dfrac{1}{7} \times \dfrac{7}{1} = \dfrac{7}{7} = 1$ the reciprocal of $\dfrac{1}{7}$ is $\dfrac{7}{1}$.

c. Since $\dfrac{5}{6} \times \dfrac{6}{5} = \dfrac{30}{30} = 1$ the reciprocal of $\dfrac{5}{6}$ is $\dfrac{6}{5}$.

To divide by a fraction you **must multiply by its reciprocal.**

DIVIDING FRACTIONS

For any numbers *a*, *b*, *c* and *d*:

$$\frac{a}{b} \div \frac{c}{d} = \frac{a}{b} \times \frac{d}{c}$$

EXAMPLE 2

Find the value of $\frac{1}{2} \div \frac{2}{3}$.

Find the reciprocal of the divisor.

$$\frac{2}{3} \rightarrow \boxed{\frac{3}{2}} \text{ because } \frac{2}{3} \times \frac{3}{2} = 1$$

Multiply the dividend by the reciprocal of the divisor.

$$\frac{1}{2} \div \frac{2}{3} = \frac{1}{2} \times \frac{3}{2} = \frac{1 \times 3}{2 \times 2} = \frac{3}{4}$$

$$\frac{1}{2} \div \frac{2}{3} = \frac{3}{4}$$

EXAMPLE 3

Yvette climbed $\frac{1}{2}$ the stairs at her house. Each stair was $\frac{1}{14}$ of the staircase. How many stairs had she climbed?

Write the problem.

$$\frac{1}{2} \div \frac{1}{14}$$

Find the reciprocal of the divisor.

$$\frac{1}{14} \rightarrow \boxed{\frac{14}{1}} \text{ because } \frac{1}{14} \times \frac{14}{1} = \frac{14}{14} = 1$$

Multiply the dividend by the reciprocal of the divisor.

$$\frac{1}{2} \div \frac{1}{14} = \frac{1}{2} \times \frac{14}{1} = \frac{1 \times 14}{2 \times 1} = \frac{14}{2} = 7$$

☑ Check using a model.

Yvette had climbed 7 stairs.

EXAMPLE 4

At the beginning of this lesson you saw a drawing of the model for $\frac{1}{2} \div \frac{3}{8}$. Find this quotient.

Find the reciprocal of the divisor.

$$\frac{3}{8} \rightarrow \frac{8}{3} \text{ because } \frac{3}{8} \times \frac{8}{3} = \frac{24}{24} = 1$$

Multiply the dividend by the divisor's reciprocal.

$$\frac{1}{2} \div \frac{3}{8} = \frac{1}{2} \times \frac{8}{3} = \frac{1 \times 8}{2 \times 3} = \frac{8}{6}$$

Simplify.

$$\frac{8}{6} = \frac{4}{3} = 1\frac{1}{3}$$

☑ Check using the model.

$$\frac{1}{2} \div \frac{3}{8} = 1\frac{1}{3}$$

Notice how the model shows the correct answer. There are $1\frac{1}{3}$ red sections circled.

EXERCISES

Find each quotient. Write your answer in simplest form.

1. $\dfrac{2}{3} \div \dfrac{1}{3}$

2. $\dfrac{6}{7} \div \dfrac{3}{7}$

3. $\dfrac{2}{5} \div \dfrac{1}{10}$

4. $\dfrac{1}{2} \div \dfrac{1}{16}$

5. $\dfrac{4}{5} \div \dfrac{2}{15}$

6. $\dfrac{7}{8} \div \dfrac{1}{8}$

7. $\dfrac{1}{2} \div \dfrac{1}{8}$

8. $\dfrac{3}{4} \div \dfrac{2}{8}$

9. $\dfrac{2}{3} \div \dfrac{2}{9}$

10. Shiloh drives $\frac{3}{4}$ mile to school each day. There is a stop sign every $\frac{3}{8}$ mile. How many times does Shiloh have to stop on her way to school?

11. When measuring ingredients:
   a. How many $\frac{1}{4}$ teaspoons make $\frac{1}{2}$ teaspoon?
   b. How many $\frac{1}{3}$ cups make $\frac{2}{3}$ cup?
   c. How many $\frac{1}{8}$ teaspoons make $\frac{1}{2}$ teaspoon?
   d. How many $\frac{1}{8}$ cups make $\frac{3}{4}$ cup?

Find each quotient. Write your answer in simplest form.

12. $\dfrac{4}{9} \div \dfrac{2}{3}$

13. $\dfrac{5}{7} \div \dfrac{1}{2}$

14. $\dfrac{5}{6} \div \dfrac{1}{5}$

15. $\dfrac{5}{9} \div \dfrac{1}{3}$

16. $\dfrac{4}{5} \div \dfrac{1}{3}$

17. $\dfrac{6}{7} \div \dfrac{3}{5}$

18. $\dfrac{1}{2} \div \dfrac{4}{5}$

19. $\dfrac{3}{4} \div \dfrac{1}{2}$

20. $\dfrac{2}{3} \div \dfrac{1}{2}$

21. Stefan has a board $\frac{2}{3}$ foot thick. He cuts $\frac{1}{8}$ foot thick sections out of it. How many sections will he cut?

22. Three-fourths of a cake remains after a birthday party. Each serving is $\frac{1}{16}$ of the cake. How many servings remain?

Write a division equation that matches each model.

23. 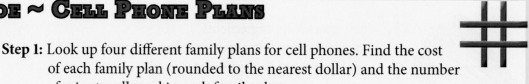 ____ ÷ ____ = ____

24. ____ ÷ ____ = ____

Find each sum or difference.

25. $\dfrac{3}{8} + \dfrac{1}{2}$

26. $\dfrac{7}{9} - \dfrac{1}{3}$

27. $4\frac{2}{5} + 1\frac{1}{3}$

28. $7\frac{1}{3} - 4\frac{1}{4}$

TIC-TAC-TOE ~ CELL PHONE PLANS

Step 1: Look up four different family plans for cell phones. Find the cost of each family plan (rounded to the nearest dollar) and the number of minutes allowed in each family plan.

Step 2: Figure out the fraction each person in your family represents.

Example: There are five people in your family. The total number would be the denominator. Each person would be the numerator. Each person represents $\frac{1}{5}$.

Step 3: Multiply the fraction that represents one person by the total minutes in each cell phone plan. This is the number of minutes you would have if the total minutes were divided evenly among family members.

Step 4: Multiply the fraction that represents one person by the total price of each family plan (rounded to the nearest dollar) to find how much each plan costs per person.

Step 5: Create a poster to display your results. Choose the plan that you think is the best. Include your reasons for choosing that plan on the poster.

ESTIMATING PRODUCTS AND QUOTIENTS

 Estimate products and quotients using compatible numbers.

Finding exact answers to problems involving multiplying and dividing fractions takes time and requires the use of paper and pencil. You may not have these things available to you in many real-world situations. **Compatible numbers** are very important when estimating products and quotients. Compatible numbers are numbers that are easy to mentally compute.

EXPLORE! 4-H CLUB

The Barnyard Critters 4-H Club held a fundraiser for their club. Each member raised money separately. The club leader collected all of the money. The pie chart to the right shows the fraction of the money spent on each type of animal the club members raise.

Barnyard Critters 4-H Club

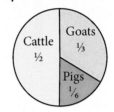

Step 1: Parrish collected $28 during the fundraiser. He wants to determine the amount of his money that was spent on goats.
  a. What calculation could Parrish do to find the exact answer?
  b. Parrish wants to determine the answer in his head. He changed the amount he collected to a number that is compatible with $\frac{1}{3}$. Which number, 27 or 29, is more compatible with $\frac{1}{3}$? Why?
  c. Use this number to determine the approximate amount of Parrish's funds spent on goats.

Step 2: Nichole raised $35. She wants to determine the amount of her money that will be spent on pigs.
  a. What calculation could Nichole do to find the exact answer?
  b. Nichole calculated the answer in her head. Which number (34 or 36) is more compatible with $\frac{1}{6}$? Why?
  c. Use this number to determine the approximate amount of Nichole's funds spent on pigs.

Step 3: The club members raised $149 overall. Approximate the amount of money spent on cows using a compatible number. What number did you choose and why?

Step 4: Use your answer from **Step 3.** Which statement would best express your answer and why?
  "The 4-H Club will spend a little less than $_____ on cows."
  "The 4-H Club will spend a little more than $_____ on cows."

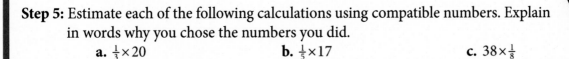

Step 5: Estimate each of the following calculations using compatible numbers. Explain in words why you chose the numbers you did.
  a. $\frac{1}{3} \times 20$ **b.** $\frac{1}{5} \times 17$ **c.** $38 \times \frac{1}{8}$

Step 6: Give a real-world situation where compatible numbers can be used to multiply. Make up an example for that situation. Estimate the solution to your situation using compatible numbers.

ESTIMATING USING COMPATIBLE NUMBERS

1. Substitute compatible numbers for one or more whole numbers or mixed numbers in the expression.
2. Find the value of the expression using the compatible numbers.

EXAMPLE 1

SOLUTION

Estimate the value of $\frac{1}{6} \times 20$.

The number 20 cannot be equally divided into sixths.

List the factors of 6.

6: 6, 12, 18, 24, 30 …

> 18 is the closest multiple of 6

Substitute the closest compatible number for 20 that is a multiple of 6. Find the value of $\frac{1}{6} \times 18$ by dividing 18 into 6 equal amounts.

$\frac{1}{6} \times 20$
↓
$\frac{1}{6} \times 18 = 3$

$\frac{1}{6} \times 20 \approx 3$

Estimate products or quotients with two mixed numbers by substituting whole compatible numbers for the mixed numbers.

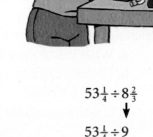

EXAMPLE 2

Johanna has a $53\frac{1}{4}$ **inch long piece of tubing for her science project. The project directions suggest cutting the tubing into** $8\frac{2}{3}$ **inch long pieces. About how many pieces will she be able to cut?**

SOLUTION

Write the problem.

$53\frac{1}{4} \div 8\frac{2}{3}$
↓

Round the divisor to the nearest whole number.

$53\frac{1}{4} \div 9$
↓

Change the dividend to the nearest multiple of the new divisor.

$54 \div 9 = 6$

Johanna will be able to cut approximately 6 pieces of tubing.

EXAMPLE 3

Jack needed about $5\frac{3}{4}$ cups of dirt for each pot he was filling. He had $4\frac{1}{4}$ pots left to fill. Approximately how much dirt does he still need?

SOLUTION

Use compatible numbers to estimate.

Choose compatible numbers for each mixed number.

Solve the problem.

$5\frac{3}{4} \times 4\frac{1}{4}$

$\downarrow \quad \downarrow$

6×4

$6 \times 4 = 24$, so $5\frac{3}{4} \times 4\frac{1}{4} \approx 24$.

Jack still needs approximately 24 cups of dirt.

EXERCISES

1. Estimating is very useful in many situations.
   a. Describe one situation where you would use estimation rather than determining the exact answer.
   b. Describe one situation where you would NOT use estimation and only an exact answer would be appropriate.

2. Define "compatible number" in your own words.

Estimate each product using compatible numbers.

3. $\frac{1}{2} \times 23$

4. $\frac{1}{4} \times 15$

5. $\frac{2}{3} \times 19$

6. $\frac{1}{6} \times 47$

7. $\frac{3}{8} \times 17$

8. $\frac{2}{5} \times 11$

9. Aisha hit 46 pitches in batting practice. One-third of the hits were fly balls. About how many hits were fly balls?

10. Jeb bought 37 tickets for the carnival. He gave $\frac{1}{6}$ of the tickets to his brother. Approximately how many tickets did Jeb's brother get?

Estimate each product using compatible numbers.

11. $6\frac{1}{4} \times 3\frac{1}{8}$

12. $5\frac{1}{9} \times 5\frac{6}{7}$

13. $4\frac{3}{10} \times 6\frac{5}{6}$

14. $9\frac{1}{12} \times 2\frac{7}{9}$

15. $7\frac{2}{11} \times 2\frac{1}{5}$

16. $3\frac{13}{15} \times 2\frac{2}{9}$

Estimate each quotient using compatible numbers.

17. $4\frac{1}{5} \div 1\frac{5}{6}$

18. $20\frac{7}{9} \div 2\frac{7}{8}$

19. $44\frac{3}{4} \div 5\frac{2}{17}$

20. $61\frac{1}{8} \div 10\frac{2}{15}$

21. $43\frac{1}{4} \div 6\frac{4}{5}$

22. $80\frac{1}{4} \div 9\frac{1}{7}$

23. Eric was a camp chef. He had $27\frac{7}{9}$ gallons of milk in the refrigerator. He used about $3\frac{5}{8}$ gallons per day. Approximately how many days will pass before he runs out of milk?

24. Zohar took $35\frac{3}{4}$ dollars from his bank account. He spent $4\frac{1}{5}$ dollars on Tuesday. He continues spending about the same amount each day. About how many days will it be until he needs to get more money?

25. Mica followed a jam recipe that called for $5\frac{1}{4}$ cups of sugar. She wanted to make $5\frac{3}{4}$ batches of jam. About how much sugar would she need?

26. Joel was filling containers with cement. Each container held about $9\frac{1}{8}$ scoops of cement. He had $6\frac{8}{9}$ containers left to fill. Estimate how much cement he needs to fill the rest of the containers.

REVIEW

Write each product in simplest form.

27. $\frac{1}{2} \times \frac{3}{4}$

28. $\frac{1}{3} \times \frac{3}{6}$

29. $\frac{2}{5} \times \frac{7}{8}$

Write each quotient in simplest form.

30. $\frac{7}{8} \div \frac{1}{2}$

31. $\frac{1}{2} \div \frac{1}{4}$

32. $\frac{5}{6} \div \frac{5}{8}$

TIC-TAC-TOE ~ FRACTION BINGO

Design a fraction Bingo game where players must correctly multiply or divide fractions.

Step 1: Create 65 fraction multiplication or division problems which have different answers.

Step 2: Use the 65 products or quotients from these problems to fill in at least ten Bingo cards with 25 spaces. Put a "free space" in the center space.

Step 3: Write a set of directions for your game. Bring the game to math class to play.

MULTIPLYING AND DIVIDING FRACTIONS AND WHOLE NUMBERS

LESSON 18

Find products or quotients of expressions that include fractions and whole numbers.

J'Marcus was up to bat nine times in his last two baseball games. One-third of his at-bats were hits. He wanted to determine how many hits he had during his nine at-bats. He must find the value of $\frac{1}{3} \times 9$ in order to find the answer. J'Marcus did this by drawing a model.

Each ball represents one of his nine at-bats.

He circled $\frac{1}{3}$ of the balls.

J'Marcus had hits in 3 of his 9 at-bats.

You can multiply or divide fractions and whole numbers using models. You can also follow the procedures you learned earlier in this Block to find the product or quotient. Before multiplying or dividing, you must write the whole number as a fraction.

A whole number can be written as a fraction by putting a 1 in the denominator. Two examples are shown below.

$$9 = \frac{9}{1} \qquad 15 = \frac{15}{1}$$

J'Marcus could have found how many hits he had in his last nine at bats by multiplying $\frac{1}{3} \times \frac{9}{1}$.

$$\frac{1}{3} \times \frac{9}{1} = \frac{1 \times 9}{3 \times 1} = \frac{9}{3} = 3$$

MULTIPLYING OR DIVIDING FRACTIONS AND WHOLE NUMBERS

1. Write the whole number as a fraction with a denominator of 1.
2. Multiply or divide.
3. Write the answer in simplest form.

EXAMPLE 1

Five-eighths of Michael's pitches in his last baseball game were strikes. If he threw 88 pitches, how many of these were strikes?

SOLUTION

Write the problem.

$$\frac{5}{8} \times 88$$

Write the whole number as a fraction.

$$\frac{5}{8} \times \frac{88}{1}$$

Multiply the fraction.

$$\frac{5}{8} \times \frac{88}{1} = \frac{5 \times \overset{11}{\cancel{88}}}{\underset{1}{\cancel{8}} \times 1} = \frac{55}{1} = 55$$

Fifty-five of Michael's pitches were strikes.

EXAMPLE 2

Find $7 \div \dfrac{3}{5}$.

SOLUTION

Write the whole number as a fraction.

$$\frac{7}{1} \div \frac{3}{5}$$

Divide.

$$\frac{7}{1} \div \frac{3}{5} = \frac{7}{1} \times \frac{5}{3} = \frac{7 \times 5}{1 \times 3} = \frac{35}{3} = 11\frac{2}{3}$$

$$7 \div \frac{3}{5} = 11\frac{2}{3}$$

EXAMPLE 3

Kaelani needed 3 cups of chocolate chips to make cookies. She only had a $\frac{1}{4}$ cup measure. How many $\frac{1}{4}$ cup measures would she need to make 3 cups?

SOLUTION

Write the problem.

$$3 \div \frac{1}{4}$$

Model.

Write the whole number as a fraction.

$$\frac{3}{1} \div \frac{1}{4}$$

Divide.

$$\frac{3}{1} \div \frac{1}{4} = \frac{3}{1} \times \frac{4}{1} = \frac{3 \times 4}{1 \times 1} = \frac{12}{1} = 12$$

Kaelani needs twelve $\frac{1}{4}$ cup measures of chocolate chips to equal 3 cups.

EXERCISES

Find each product.

1. $\frac{1}{4} \times 16$

2. $\frac{2}{3} \times 15$

3. $\frac{5}{6} \times 18$

4. $\frac{3}{7} \times 20$

5. $\frac{4}{9} \times 12$

6. $\frac{3}{4} \times 11$

7. The short track speed skating was dominated by South Korea in the 2006 winter Olympics at Torino, Italy. They took $\frac{5}{12}$ of the 24 medals awarded. How many medals did South Korea win?

8. Southern Oregon University's 2006-2007 men's basketball team won $\frac{2}{5}$ of their 30 games. How many games did they win?

9. Stacia washed windows at an office building. She had 24 windows to wash. At three o'clock Stacia had washed $\frac{4}{5}$ of the windows. How many windows had she washed so far?

10. A math teacher had 29 homework assignments to correct. She had corrected $\frac{3}{4}$ of the homework before she went home. How many assignments had she corrected?

Find each quotient.

11. $5 \div \frac{1}{2}$

12. $6 \div \frac{3}{4}$

13. $9 \div \frac{3}{5}$

14. $7 \div \frac{3}{4}$

15. $8 \div \frac{2}{3}$

16. $3 \div \frac{2}{7}$

17. Jessamyn ordered five pizzas. Jessamyn ordered enough so that each person at her party could eat $\frac{1}{3}$ of a pizza. How many people did she serve?

18. Jed bought six small bags of candy for his class. Each person received $\frac{1}{4}$ of a bag of candy. How many people got candy?

19. It took 15 gallons of gasoline to fill Reggie's gas tank. Reggie said his car used $\frac{2}{3}$ gallon of gas to drive to work and back. How many trips to work and back could Reggie make on one tank of gas?

20. Marita uses $\frac{3}{4}$ of a jalapeno pepper for each batch of fresh salsa. She has 13 jalapeno peppers. How many batches of salsa can she make?

Measure the sides of each polygon with a customary ruler. Find each perimeter.

21.

22.

23.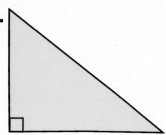

Estimate each product or quotient using compatible numbers.

24. $33 \div 8\frac{1}{8}$

25. $17 \div 3\frac{1}{3}$

26. $4\frac{2}{3} \times 8\frac{5}{6}$

27. $9\frac{4}{7} \div 2\frac{1}{8}$

28. $11\frac{1}{12} \times 3\frac{5}{7}$

29. $203 \div 19\frac{1}{9}$

TIC-TAC-TOE ~ HOW MANY MINUTES?

Karen spent $\frac{2}{3}$ hour practicing piano. She practiced a song called "Jazz Time" for $\frac{1}{2}$ of this time. How many minutes did she spend practicing "Jazz Time"?

Multiply the two fractions to figure out the fraction of an hour she spent practicing "Jazz Time."

Example: $\frac{1}{2} \times \frac{2}{3} = \frac{2}{6} = \frac{1}{3}$ Karen spent $\frac{1}{3}$ hour practicing "Jazz Time."

In order to figure out how many minutes Karen spent practicing this song, multiply the fraction of an hour by the number of minutes in an hour (60).

Example: $\frac{1}{3} \times 60 = 20$ Karen spent 20 minutes practicing "Jazz Time."

How many minutes are in...

1. $\frac{1}{4}$ hour?

2. $\frac{1}{6}$ hour?

3. $\frac{1}{10}$ hour?

4. $\frac{3}{4}$ hour?

5. $\frac{2}{3}$ hour?

6. $\frac{7}{12}$ hour?

7. $\frac{1}{3}$ of $\frac{1}{2}$ hour?

8. $\frac{5}{6}$ of $\frac{1}{2}$ hour?

9. $\frac{1}{3}$ of $\frac{1}{4}$ hour?

10. $\frac{1}{2}$ of $\frac{1}{6}$ hour?

11. $\frac{3}{8}$ of $\frac{2}{3}$ hour?

12. $\frac{7}{9}$ of $\frac{3}{4}$ hour?

MULTIPLYING AND DIVIDING MIXED NUMBERS

LESSON 19

 Find products and quotients of expressions that include mixed numbers.

Y ou have learned how to find the products and quotients of two fractions or a fraction and a whole number in this Block. You will learn how to find products and quotients of expressions involving mixed numbers in this lesson.

EXPLORE!   **SCRAPBOOKING**

Katelyn enjoys putting her photos into scrapbooks. When she works diligently, she completes $3\frac{1}{2}$ pages each hour.

Step 1: Katelyn's relatives are coming in $2\frac{1}{2}$ hours. Katelyn wants to know how many pages she can finish before they arrive.
> **a.** Write a math problem that will help her determine this.
> **b.** Change each mixed number to an improper fraction and calculate.
> **c.** Simplify the answer. Write it in a complete sentence.

Step 2: Katelyn plans to complete 14 pages of her scrapbook tomorrow. How many hours will it take her?
> **a.** Write the problem.
> **b.** Change both the whole number and mixed number to fractions and calculate.
> **c.** Simplify the answer. Write the answer in a complete sentence.

Step 3: Katelyn spent a total of $9\frac{1}{3}$ hours on her scrapbook last week. How many pages did she complete?

Step 4: Stephen is just learning to scrapbook. He can finish $2\frac{3}{4}$ pages each hour. He worked with Katelyn for the entire $9\frac{1}{3}$ hours last week. How many pages did he complete?

Step 5: Describe in words the steps to take when multiplying or dividing two mixed numbers.

MULTIPLYING AND DIVIDING MIXED NUMBERS

1. Write each mixed or whole number as a fraction.
2. Multiply or divide using the improper fractions.
3. Write the answer in simplest form.

EXAMPLE 1   **Find the value of $7\frac{1}{3} \times 1\frac{1}{4}$.**

SOLUTION   Change each mixed number to an improper fraction.

$$7\frac{1}{3} = \frac{22}{3}$$
$$1\frac{1}{4} = \frac{5}{4}$$

Rewrite and multiply.

$$\frac{\overset{11}{\cancel{22}}}{3} \times \frac{5}{\underset{2}{\cancel{4}}} = \frac{55}{6}$$

Write as a mixed number.

$$\frac{55}{6} = 9\frac{1}{6}$$

$$7\frac{1}{3} \times 1\frac{1}{4} = 9\frac{1}{6}$$

EXAMPLE 2   **Brennan bought $7\frac{3}{8}$ pounds of salmon for his family. Each portion was about $\frac{1}{2}$ pound of salmon. How many portions could he serve?**

SOLUTION   Write the problem.

$$7\frac{3}{8} \div \frac{1}{2}$$

Write the mixed number as an improper fraction.

$$7\frac{3}{8} = \frac{59}{8}$$

Divide.

$$\frac{59}{8} \div \frac{1}{2} = \frac{59}{8} \times \frac{2}{1} = \frac{59 \times 2}{8 \times 1} = \frac{118}{8} = 14\frac{6}{8}$$

Simplify.

$$14\frac{6}{8} = 14\frac{3}{4}$$

Brennan could serve $14\frac{3}{4}$ portions of salmon.

To find the reciprocal of a whole number, write the whole number as a fraction over 1. Then "flip" the fraction.

$$3 = \frac{3}{1} \xrightarrow{\text{Reciprocal}} \frac{1}{3}$$

EXAMPLE 3   **Isaac built a tree house for his daughter. He cut a board into 5 equal pieces. How long is each piece of board if the original board was $11\frac{1}{2}$ feet long?**

SOLUTION   Write the problem.

$$11\frac{1}{2} \div 5$$

Write each whole and mixed number as an improper fraction.

$$11\frac{1}{2} = \frac{23}{2}$$
$$5 = \frac{5}{1}$$

Multiply by the reciprocal of the divisor.

$$\frac{23}{2} \div \frac{5}{1} = \frac{23}{2} \times \frac{1}{5} = \frac{23}{10}$$

Change into a mixed number.

$$\frac{23}{10} = 2\frac{3}{10}$$

Each equal piece of the board is $2\frac{3}{10}$ feet long.

EXERCISES

Find each product.

1. $2\frac{1}{8} \times 2$

2. $3 \times 2\frac{2}{9}$

3. $2\frac{1}{5} \times 5$

4. $4\frac{2}{3} \times \frac{4}{5}$

5. $\frac{1}{3} \times 3\frac{3}{8}$

6. $\frac{5}{6} \times 2\frac{1}{3}$

7. $2\frac{2}{5} \times 1\frac{2}{3}$

8. $1\frac{1}{6} \times 3\frac{1}{2}$

9. $5\frac{1}{2} \times 1\frac{2}{3}$

10. Naomi used $4\frac{3}{4}$ tablespoons of ground coffee for each pot of coffee she made. She made one pot of coffee each day, Monday through Friday. How many tablespoons of ground coffee did she use altogether?

11. Yani made cookies. He used $2\frac{1}{4}$ cups of flour per batch of cookies. He made $3\frac{1}{2}$ batches of cookies. How much flour did he use?

Find each quotient.

12. $6\frac{2}{5} \div 2$

13. $5 \div 1\frac{1}{4}$

14. $9\frac{2}{5} \div 3$

15. $3\frac{1}{9} \div \frac{1}{3}$

16. $2\frac{5}{6} \div \frac{3}{8}$

17. $4\frac{1}{6} \div \frac{3}{4}$

18. $6\frac{8}{9} \div 2\frac{1}{3}$

19. $3\frac{1}{2} \div 1\frac{1}{4}$

20. $5\frac{1}{3} \div 1\frac{2}{3}$

21. Ty edged a flower bed with paving stones. Each paving stone was $5\frac{3}{4}$ inches long. The length of the flower bed was $40\frac{1}{4}$ inches long. How many paving stones did Ty need?

22. J.D. built a tower out of blocks with his nephew. Each block was $1\frac{3}{4}$ inches tall. They built a $43\frac{3}{4}$ inch tall tower . How many blocks did they use?

REVIEW

Find each sum or difference.

23. $\frac{4}{5} - \frac{1}{2}$

24. $\frac{3}{4} + \frac{1}{8}$

25. $\frac{1}{2} - \frac{3}{7}$

Find each product or quotient.

26. $3 \times \frac{2}{3}$

27. $\frac{14}{15} \div \frac{1}{5}$

28. $9 \times \frac{4}{5}$

29. $8 \div \frac{3}{4}$

30. $\frac{2}{3} \times \frac{9}{10}$

31. $11 \div \frac{2}{3}$

TIC-TAC-TOE ~ ADVERTISEMENTS

Step 1: Look online or in a newspaper for "Buy One, Get One Half Off" advertisements. Find at least five different advertisements. Print them or cut them out.

Step 2: Choose an item from one advertisement.

Step 3: Record the price of the first item (full price). Round to the nearest dollar.

Step 4: Record the price of the second identical item (half-off price). Round to the nearest dollar.

Step 5: Find the price per item by averaging the two prices $\dfrac{\text{full price} + \text{half price}}{2}$.

Step 6: Repeat **Steps 2-5** for four more items from different advertisements.

Step 7: Use the advertisements and your calculations to make a collage. Display the advertisements, the price of one item, the price of the second item at half-off, and the average price per item.

TIC-TAC-TOE ~ CHANGING RECIPES

Step 1: Choose a favorite recipe with at least five ingredients.

Step 2: Find the amounts of ingredients needed to cut the recipe in half. Rewrite the recipe using your results.

Step 3: Figure out the ingredient amounts you would need for $1\frac{1}{2}$ times the recipe. Rewrite the recipe using your results.

Step 4: Rewrite the recipe tripling the ingredients.

AREA WITH FRACTIONS

Calculate areas of rectangles, squares and triangles with lengths of sides that are fractions or mixed numbers.

A builder needs to know how many square feet of siding to buy for one side of a house. A carpet layer needs to know the square footage of a room so carpet can be ordered. An architect finds the square footage on blueprints in order to give final dimensions to the owner of a company wishing to build a new office building.

Area is the number of square units used to cover a surface. A rectangle with an area of 6 square units can also be written as 6 units².

2 units — 6 units² — **Six square units cover the surface of the rectangle.**

3 units

How do the length and width affect the area? One side is 2 units. The other side is 3 units. The area is 6 square units. $2 \times 3 = 6$

The area of different **shapes can be found using multiplication.**

AREA OF A RECTANGLE

Area = *length × width*

width

length

EXAMPLE 1

Find the area of the rectangle.

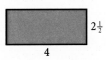 $2\frac{1}{2}$

4

SOLUTION

Area = *length × width*   Area = $4 \times 2\frac{1}{2}$

Change the mixed number and whole number into improper fractions. $4 = \frac{4}{1}$ and $2\frac{1}{2} = \frac{5}{2}$

Multiply.   Area $= \frac{4}{1} \times \frac{5}{2} = \frac{20}{2}$ or $\overset{2}{\cancel{4}}{\vphantom{1}}_{1} \times \frac{5}{\cancel{2}} = \frac{10}{1}$

Simplify. $\frac{20}{2} = 10$ or $\frac{10}{1} = 10$

The area of the rectangle is 10 square units or 10 units².

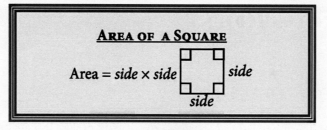

AREA OF A SQUARE

Area = *side* × *side*   *side*

side

EXAMPLE 2

Find the area of the square. $1\frac{1}{2} ft$

SOLUTION

Area = *side* × *side*   Area $= 1\frac{1}{2} \times 1\frac{1}{2}$

Change mixed numbers to improper fractions. $1\frac{1}{2} = \frac{3}{2}$

Multiply.   Area $= \frac{3}{2} \times \frac{3}{2} = \frac{9}{4}$

Simplify. $\frac{9}{4} = 2\frac{1}{4}$

The area of the square is $2\frac{1}{4}$ square feet or $2\frac{1}{4} ft^2$.

EXPLORE!   **TRIANGLE AREA**

Step 1: Draw a rectangle on grid paper.

Step 2: Count the number of grid squares that make up the rectangle's area. Write this to the side of the rectangle as Area = ___ square units.

Step 3: Record the rectangle's length and width. Label these on the outside of the rectangle.

Step 4: Draw a diagonal line from one corner of the rectangle to the opposite corner to make a right triangle.

Step 5: What do you think is the area of each triangle formed? Explain your reasoning.

The length of the base and the height are used when finding the area of a triangle. The height of a triangle is a perpendicular line segment drawn from the base of the triangle to the opposite vertex. The base and height are perpendicular if they form a right angle where the two line segments meet.

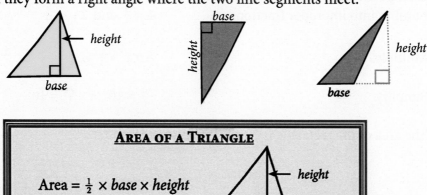

AREA OF A TRIANGLE

Area = $\frac{1}{2}$ × *base* × *height*   *height*

base

EXAMPLE 3

Find the area of the triangle.

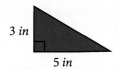

3 in

5 in

SOLUTION

Area = $\frac{1}{2}$ × *base* × *height*   Area = $\frac{1}{2}$ × 5 × 3

Change the whole numbers into fractions.   5 = $\frac{5}{1}$ and 3 = $\frac{3}{1}$

Multiply.   Area = $\frac{1}{2}$ × $\frac{5}{1}$ × $\frac{3}{1}$ = $\frac{15}{2}$

Simplify.   Area = $\frac{15}{2}$ = $7\frac{1}{2}$

The area of the triangle is $7\frac{1}{2}$ square inches or $7\frac{1}{2}$ in^2.

EXERCISES

Use the given measurements to find the area of each rectangle.

1.
2 units

5 units

2.
$3\frac{1}{2}$ units

3 units

3.
$2\frac{1}{4}$ units

$3\frac{3}{4}$ units

4.
$\frac{7}{8}$ in

$\frac{5}{8}$ in

5.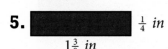
$\frac{1}{4}$ in

$1\frac{3}{8}$ in

6.
$1\frac{9}{16}$ in

$\frac{3}{4}$ in

 7. A carpet layer measured the floor in a room to be carpeted. The room was $20\frac{1}{3}$ ft long and $18\frac{3}{4}$ ft wide. What is the area of the floor in this room?

Use the given measurement to find the area of each square.

8.
4 units

9.
$2\frac{1}{3}$ units

10.

11.
$3\frac{3}{4}$ in

12.
$1\frac{1}{8}$ in

$6\frac{1}{2}$ in

13. Estaban has an end table with a square top. One side of the top of the table is $2\frac{7}{8}$ ft long. What is the area of the top of Estaban's table?

Find the area of the triangles using the given heights and bases.

14.

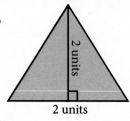

2 units

2 units

15.

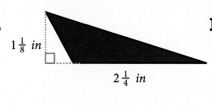

$1\frac{1}{8}$ in

$2\frac{1}{4}$ in

16.

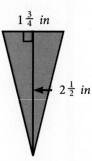

$1\frac{3}{4}$ in

$2\frac{1}{2}$ in

 Measure the sides of the following polygons with a customary ruler to the nearest quarter inch. Find the area of each polygon.

17.

18.

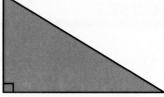

19.

20.

21.

22.

23. Two rectangles each have an area of 12 inches. Find the dimensions of two different rectangles that fit this description.

24. Two triangles each have an area of 12 inches. Find the dimensions of two rectangles that fit this description.

REVIEW

Find each product.

25. $3\frac{1}{3} \times \frac{5}{6}$

26. $2\frac{1}{9} \times 2\frac{3}{4}$

27. $5\frac{1}{2} \times 2$

Find each quotient.

28. $6\frac{1}{5} \div \frac{2}{3}$

29. $2\frac{5}{7} \div 1\frac{1}{2}$

30. $7\frac{7}{8} \div 2\frac{1}{5}$

TIC-TAC-TOE ~ LANDSCAPING

Step 1: Draw your own backyard landscape with flower beds, or design one. Write the measurements, to the nearest inch, on all sides of each flower bed. Measure your own back yard or check your design measurements with an adult to make sure the measurements are realistic.

Step 2: Use advertisements, the internet or information from a home or garden store to choose an edging block to outline each flower bed. Record a drawing of the edging block and the real length.

Step 3: How many edging blocks do you need to edge the perimeter of each flower bed in your landscape design?

Step 4: How many edging blocks do you need altogether?

Step 5: What is the total cost for the edging blocks?

Step 6: Display the landscape on a poster. Include the source of your materials along with **Steps 1-5** on your poster. Show your calculations on a separate sheet of paper.

TIC-TAC-TOE ~ DREAM HOUSE

Step 1: Use grid paper to draw a one-story dream house where each square equals $2\frac{1}{2}$ feet. You must have at least 6 rooms. Make sure at least three rooms have an odd number of squares on the length and/or width.

Example:

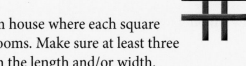

Game room = $12\frac{1}{2} ft \times 15 ft$

$$\frac{25}{2} \times \frac{15}{1} = \frac{375}{2} = 187\frac{1}{2} ft^2$$

Step 2: Figure out the square footage of each room.

Step 3: Calculate the square footage of the entire house.

Vocabulary

area	divisor	quotient
compatible numbers	dividend	reciprocal
	perpendicular	

 Use models to multiply fractions.
Find products of expressions involving two fractions.
Use models to divide fractions.
Find quotients of expressions involving two fractions.
Estimate products and quotients using compatible numbers.
Find products or quotients of expressions that include fractions and whole numbers.
Find products and quotients of expressions that include mixed numbers.
Calculate areas of rectangles, squares and triangles with lengths of sides that are fractions or mixed numbers.

Lesson 13 ~ Multiplying Fractions with Models

Write an equation to match each model.

1.

2.

3.

Draw a model to represent each expression. Write the answer to the expression.

4. $\dfrac{1}{4} \times \dfrac{1}{2}$

5. $\dfrac{1}{2} \times \dfrac{2}{5}$

6. $\dfrac{2}{3} \times \dfrac{1}{4}$

Lesson 14 ~ Multiplying Fractions

Find each product. Write your answer in simplest form.

7. $\dfrac{2}{3} \times \dfrac{3}{8}$

8. $\dfrac{7}{8} \times \dfrac{1}{4}$

9. $\dfrac{5}{6} \times \dfrac{2}{3}$

10. $\dfrac{4}{5} \times \dfrac{1}{8}$

11. $\dfrac{1}{2} \times \dfrac{3}{5}$

12. $\dfrac{5}{9} \times \dfrac{1}{5}$

13. Izaya washed $\frac{1}{3}$ of the cars at the car wash. Todd washed $\frac{3}{8}$ as many as Izaya washed. What fraction of the total cars did Todd wash?

14. Cindy buys $\frac{1}{3}$ yard of fabric. She only needs $\frac{2}{3}$ of this fabric for the project she's making. What fraction of a yard will she use?

15. Nadine ate $\frac{1}{4}$ of a basket of chicken. Suzanne ate $\frac{1}{3}$ of the amount that Nadine ate. What fraction of the basket of chicken did Suzanne eat?

Lesson 15 ~ Dividing Fractions with Models
• •

Write an equation to match each model.

16.

17.

18.

Draw a model to represent each expression. Write the answer to the equation.

19. $\frac{3}{8} \div \frac{1}{8}$

20. $\frac{4}{5} \div \frac{2}{5}$

21. $\frac{2}{3} \div \frac{1}{6}$

Lesson 16 ~ Dividing Fractions
• •

Find each quotient. Write your answer in simplest form.

22. $\frac{4}{5} \div \frac{1}{5}$

23. $\frac{1}{2} \div \frac{1}{8}$

24. $\frac{4}{5} \div \frac{1}{10}$

25. $\frac{3}{7} \div \frac{1}{2}$

26. $\frac{5}{6} \div \frac{1}{8}$

27. $\frac{3}{5} \div \frac{2}{3}$

28. Jordyn has $\frac{7}{8}$ of a liter of water. She has bottles that each hold $\frac{1}{2}$ liter of water. How many bottles can she fill?

29. Evie drives $\frac{2}{3}$ mile to work each day. She sees students waiting at bus stops every $\frac{1}{6}$ mile. How many times does she pass students waiting at bus stops on one trip to work?

30. Joseph put $\frac{3}{4}$ gallon of marinara sauce into jars. Each jar holds $\frac{1}{8}$ gallon. How many jars of marinara sauce does Joseph have?

Lesson 17 ~ Estimating Products and Quotients

Estimate each product or quotient.

31. $\frac{1}{2} \times 21$

32. $28\frac{1}{6} \div 4\frac{1}{3}$

33. $\frac{1}{8} \times 17$

34. $16\frac{1}{9} \div 5\frac{2}{11}$

35. $71\frac{4}{9} \div 8\frac{2}{9}$

36. $5\frac{1}{10} \times 3\frac{1}{3}$

37. Tamira entered a relay race where the team must swim a total of $35\frac{1}{8}$ laps. The four members of the team each swam equal distances in the race. About how many laps did each relay team member swim?

38. Nathaniel had 17 carrot sticks. He gave $\frac{1}{4}$ of the carrot sticks to his brother. Approximately how many carrot sticks did his brother get?

Lesson 18 ~ Multiplying and Dividing Fractions and Whole Numbers

Find each product or quotient. Write in simplest form.

39. $\frac{1}{8} \times 64$

40. $\frac{2}{5} \times 20$

41. $9 \div \frac{3}{4}$

42. $15 \div \frac{3}{5}$

43. $\frac{3}{4} \times 34$

44. $32 \div \frac{2}{3}$

45. $25 \div \frac{5}{8}$

46. $\frac{1}{5} \times 22$

47. $12 \times \frac{2}{5}$

48. Mrs. Jenkins tore off 7 pieces of butcher paper to decorate her bulletin boards. Each piece of paper was $\frac{3}{4}$ of a yard long. What was the total length of paper she tore off?

Lesson 19 ~ Multiplying and Dividing Mixed Numbers

Find each product or quotient. Write in simplest form.

49. $5\frac{1}{8} \times \frac{2}{3}$

50. $5\frac{3}{5} \div 1\frac{1}{2}$

51. $5\frac{1}{4} \div 3\frac{3}{5}$

52. $2\frac{1}{8} \div \frac{1}{3}$

53. $3\frac{4}{7} \times 1\frac{1}{3}$

54. $4\frac{2}{3} \times 2\frac{3}{4}$

55. Lani is given $21\frac{1}{2}$ dollars for lunches. She spends $3\frac{1}{4}$ dollars each day. How many days will it be until she runs out of money?

56. Sakaiya uses $4\frac{1}{4}$ cups of sugar for every batch of freezer jam. He makes $1\frac{1}{2}$ batches of jam. How many cups of sugar does he use?

Use the given measurements to find the area of the following shapes.

57.  $2\frac{1}{4}$ in
$4\frac{2}{3}$ in

58. 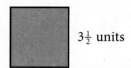 $3\frac{1}{2}$ units

59. 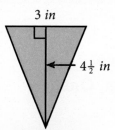 3 in
$4\frac{1}{2}$ in

60.  $3\frac{1}{3}$ units
$4\frac{1}{2}$ units

61. 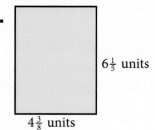 $6\frac{1}{5}$ units
$4\frac{3}{8}$ units

62.  $4\frac{1}{3}$ in

 Measure the sides of the following polygons, using an inch ruler, to the nearest sixteenth of an inch. Find the area of each polygon.

63.

64.

65.

CAREER FOCUS

JULIE
REPORTER
PORTLAND, OREGON

I am a news reporter. I talk to people to find the latest or most interesting news in my city. Then I write stories for the newspaper and the newspaper website. I also record or videotape people in the news to broadcast on the website. It is a fast-paced job. No two days are ever the same. I also know my city and state very well because reporters are always on the move looking for news.

I use math, including addition, subtraction, percentages and averages, almost every day. Numbers help me understand changes in our city, such as how many new people moved here from another state, or how many people voted for one candidate. Reporters study financial reports to understand if the businesses in our city are doing well or poorly, or if there is enough money to pay for more schools. Numbers don't lie.

I received a Bachelor of Arts degree in journalism to become a journalist. I also studied history. Some reporters study English, geology, political science or law. What we share is a common desire to take complicated information and present it in a way that people can understand. Reporters can also work for television and radio stations. Every city needs reporters. Reporters in small towns may earn $20,000 a year while those in larger cities earn $45,000 to $85,000 per year.

Being a reporter is like holding a magic key to enter any door or world you wish. I can go into a hospital operating room to write a story about a doctor, or ride in an experimental airplane. I can meet famous people. But the most important thing I do is find hidden news that, once it becomes known, makes the world a better place.

BLOCK 4 ~ FRACTIONS AND DECIMALS
DECIMALS

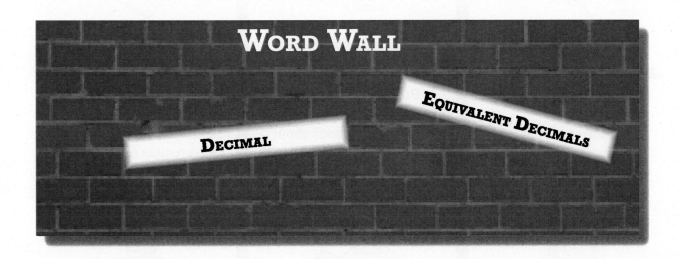

BLOCK 4 ~ DECIMALS
TIC - TAC - TOE

PURCHASE SPREADSHEET

Add and subtract purchases using a spreadsheet.

See page 131 for details.

CHECK THE NEWSPAPER

Make a display of newspaper clippings showing examples of decimal or fraction use.

See page 113 for details.

COMPOSITE FIGURES

Figure out the perimeters and areas of composite figures.

See page 150 for details.

DECIMAL POETRY

Write a poem about multiplying decimals by decimals. Write another poem about dividing decimals.

See page 141 for details.

VOCABULARY MEMORY

Create a vocabulary matching game to help students remember all the vocabulary words.

See page 113 for details.

CHECKBOOK REGISTRY

You have $300 to spend on gifts for family and friends. Record purchases in your checkbook registry.

See page 127 for details.

BEDROOM AREA

Find the area of your room and furniture in square meters. See if there are different ways to arrange the furniture.

See page 155 for details.

PLACE VALUE STORY

Write a picture book about place value. Use decimals as characters.

See page 123 for details.

LETTER TO THE EDITOR

Should the USA use metric measurement or customary measurement? Write a letter to the editor with reasons to back up your opinion.

See page 149 for details.

PLACE VALUE WITH DECIMALS

LESSON 21

Identify place value of decimals to the thousandths.

The fruit stand charges $2.75 for a pound of dried fruit. Trish bought 4.1 pounds of dried fruit. She paid $11.55 for the fruit.

2.75 ← decimal
↑
decimal point

All numbers in the situation above are decimals. A **decimal** is any base ten number written with a decimal point. Decimals are based on the number ten.

FOUR DIFFERENT WAYS TO MODEL DECIMALS

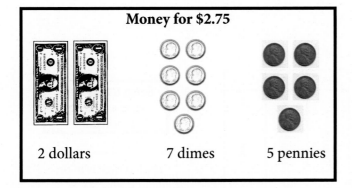

Money for $2.75

2 dollars   7 dimes   5 pennies

Place-Value Chart showing 2.75

1000	100	10	1	0.1	0.01	0.001
Thousands	Hundreds	Tens	Ones	Tenths	Hundredths	Thousandths
			2	7	5	

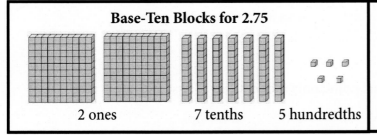

Base-Ten Blocks for 2.75

2 ones   7 tenths   5 hundredths

Decimal Models for 2.75

two   75 hundredths

The value and position of each digit in a decimal determine how much the decimal is worth. The decimal point separates the whole number from the part that is less than one.

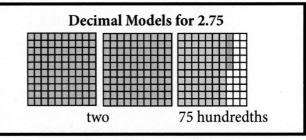

1000	100	10	1	0.1	0.01	0.001
Thousands	Hundreds	Tens	Ones	Tenths	Hundredths	Thousandths
		1	3	5	6	2

Whole Number   Less Than One

What is it worth?
The 1 represents one ten.
The 3 represents three ones.
The 5 represents five tenths.
The 6 represents six hundredths.
The 2 represents two thousandths.

To write decimals in word form, separate the whole number from the part that is less than one with the word "and." The decimal point is read as "and."

EXAMPLE 1   **Write 431.25 in word form.**

SOLUTION   Fill in the place-value chart for the number.

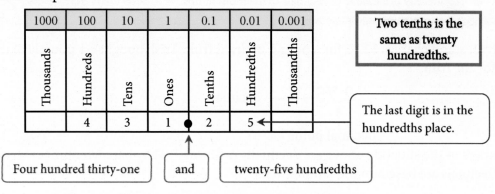

Two tenths is the same as twenty hundredths.

The last digit is in the hundredths place.

Four hundred thirty-one   and   twenty-five hundredths

EXAMPLE 2   **Write 45.703 in word form.**

SOLUTION   Fill in the place-value chart for the number.

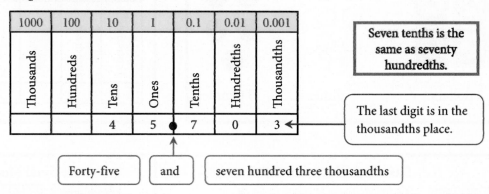

Seven tenths is the same as seventy hundredths.

The last digit is in the thousandths place.

Forty-five   and   seven hundred three thousandths

When there is no whole number preceding the decimal point, only the part that is less than one is read.

EXAMPLE 3   **Write 0.6 in word form.**

SOLUTION   Fill in the place-value chart for the number.

1000	100	10	1	0.1	0.01	0.001
Thousands	Hundreds	Tens	Ones	Tenths	Hundredths	Thousandths
			0	6		

The last digit is in the tenths place.

Six tenths

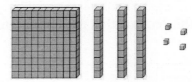

Step 1: Set out base-ten blocks for the decimal 1.34 and fill in a place-value chart. Write this number in word form. Which number is in the tenths place?

Step 2: Set out base-ten blocks for the decimal 4.51 and fill in a place-value chart. Write this number in word form. Which number is in the hundredths place?

Step 3: Set out base-ten blocks for the decimal 2.97 and fill in a place-value chart. Write this number in word form. Which number is in the hundredths place?

Step 4: Set out base-ten blocks for the decimal 5.09 and fill in a place-value chart. Write this number in word form. Which number is in the tenths place?

Step 5: Set out base-ten blocks for the decimal 3.02 and fill in a place-value chart. Write this number in word form. Which number is in the hundredths place?

Step 6: Set out base-ten blocks for the decimal 2.53 and fill in a place-value chart. Which number is in the tenths place?

Step 7: Make a model of 2.46 using base-ten blocks. Draw the base-ten blocks on the piece of paper. (Use a large square for ones, a skinny rectangle for tenths and a small square for hundredths.)

Step 8: Fill in a place-value chart with the decimal that matches your drawing.

Step 9: Write the word form for your decimal under the place-value chart.

Step 10: Repeat **Steps 7-9** for at least three decimals using ones, tenths and hundredths.

EXAMPLE 4	**Write the decimal that represents two and sixty-three hundredths.**
SOLUTION	Write the whole number. two = 2
	Insert the decimal point for 'and.' two and = 2.
	Add the part that is less than one. sixty-three hundredths = 2.63
	two and sixty-three hundredths = 2.63

EXERCISES

Write the decimal that each base-ten block group represents.

1.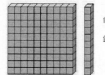

2.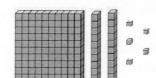

3.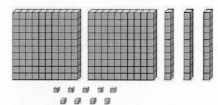

4.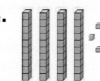

5.

6.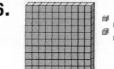

7.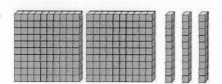

8.

9. In which place is the digit 9 in each decimal?

  a. 42.709   **b.** 9.231   **c.** 14.902   **d.** 81.493

Write the value of the underlined digit in each decimal.

10. 2.1<u>8</u>3

11. 31.20<u>8</u>

12. 7.2<u>6</u>4

13. 4<u>3</u>.56

Write a decimal to match each word form.

14. sixteen and twenty-three hundredths

15. ninety-nine and two tenths

16. three and four hundred eleven thousandths

17. fifty-two and six hundredths

18. seventy-eight and four thousandths

19. two hundred twenty-three thousandths

Write each decimal in word form.

20. 4.9

21. 35.87

22. 11.04

23. 0.549

24. 4.008

25. 68.4

REVIEW

Find each sum, difference, product or quotient.

26. $\dfrac{1}{3} + \dfrac{5}{6}$

27. $\dfrac{7}{8} - \dfrac{1}{2}$

28. $\dfrac{10}{13} \times \dfrac{2}{5}$

29. $\dfrac{14}{15} \div \dfrac{2}{3}$

30. $\dfrac{9}{10} - \dfrac{3}{5}$

31. $\dfrac{1}{4} + \dfrac{2}{3}$

Estimate each product or quotient using compatible numbers.

32. $19\frac{3}{4} \div 2\frac{1}{7}$

33. $25\frac{1}{4} \times 3\frac{1}{8}$

34. $73\frac{2}{3} \div 24\frac{1}{4}$

TIC-TAC-TOE ~ VOCABULARY MEMORY

Copy each vocabulary word from the blocks of this book onto separate cards. Copy the definition for each vocabulary word onto a different card of the same size. Create a memory game with the cards. The goal of the game is to match the word with the correct definition. Play this game in math class with your classmates to review vocabulary. Make a key showing the correct matches.

TIC-TAC-TOE ~ CHECK THE NEWSPAPER

You say "$\frac{1}{2}$ hour," (one half hour) not "0.5 hour" (point five of an hour). You say you spent $1.50, not $1\frac{1}{2}$ dollars. There are many instances that require you to write or speak using decimals or fractions. Look through several newspapers. Cut out clippings showing decimal or fraction use. Make a display showing examples where decimals are used instead of fractions.

Choose four examples. Explain why the chosen method of writing (either decimals or fractions) works for each example.

ROUNDING DECIMALS

Round decimals to the nearest one, tenth, hundredth or thousandth.

Many products are labeled with both customary and metric measurements. For example, a half gallon of milk is also labeled 1.89 liters. If you want to know how many liters equal a half gallon, you use rounding. Look at the digits that follow the one you want to round to (in this case you want to round to the ones place). You can find out ABOUT how many liters equal a half gallon. Rounding 1.89 liters to the nearest liter is 2 liters.

> ### ROUNDING DECIMALS
> 1. Underline the digit to which you will round.
> 2. Look at the digit to the right of the underlined digit.
>   - If the digit is 4 or less, the underlined numeral stays the same.
>   - If the digit is 5 or greater, add one to the underlined digit.
> 3. Rewrite the decimal. Stop after writing the rounded digit.

EXAMPLE 1

Round 0.59 to the nearest tenth.

SOLUTION

Underline the number in the tenths place.   0.5̲9

Look at the digit to the right of the underlined digit.   It is 9.

If the digit is 5 or greater, add one to the underlined digit.   5 + 1 = 6

0.59 rounded to the nearest tenth is 0.6.

EXAMPLE 2

A newborn bird weighed 2.84 ounces. How much did the bird weigh to the nearest ounce?

SOLUTION

Underline the digit you are rounding to.   2̲.84

Look at the digit to the right of the underlined digit.   It is 8.

If the digit is 5 or greater, add one to the underlined digit.   2 + 1 = 3

The baby bird weighed almost 3 ounces because 2.84 rounded to the nearest one is 3.

EXAMPLE 3

Terrell worked 15.25 hours last week. He is paid for each full hour he works. When he fills in his time card, he must fill in the hours to the nearest hour. What should he write for last week?

SOLUTION

Terrell needs to round to the nearest one.   15.25

Look at the digit to the right of the underlined digit.   It is a 2.

If the digit is 4 or less, the underlined digit stays the same.

15.25 rounded to the nearest one is 15.

Terrell needs to write 15 hours on his time card.

EXAMPLE 4

A gas station advertised the price of unleaded gas as $3.999 per gallon. Oksana said she paid $3.99 per gallon. Was she correct?

SOLUTION

Oksana needs to round to the nearest hundredth (penny).   3.999

Look at the digit to the right of the underlined digit.   It is 9.

If the digit is 5 or greater, add a one to the underlined digit.   9 + 1 = 10

Because ten is not a single digit, continue rounding digits to the left until you do not get a ten. In this case, $3.999 rounded to the nearest penny (hundredth) becomes $4.00.

Oksana is not correct. She actually paid closer to $4.00 per gallon of gas than $3.99.

EXERCISES

Round each number to the nearest one.

1. 4.3

2. 2.523

3. 6.89

4. 23.09

5. 17.99

6. 9.99

7. Joshua spent 1.75 hours texting his friends last week. To the nearest hour, how many hours did he spend texting last week?

8. A meter equals 39.37 inches. About how many inches equal one meter?

Round each number to the nearest tenth.

9. 34.91

10. 43.56

11. 71.25

12. 3.57

13. 3.908

14. 4.96

15. Maria wants to buy sheet music for $2.36. How much money should she take to buy it, to the nearest dime?

16. Aleah downloaded two music videos. They cost a total of $3.88. How much will she spend, to the nearest dime?

Round each number to the nearest hundredth.

17. 45.205

18. 1.632

19. 321.2371

20. 6.228

21. 3.904

22. 1.0962

Round each number to the nearest thousandth.

23. 7.9087

24. 50.1011

25. 201.10895

26. 1.7999

27. 5.000647

28. 11.3192

REVIEW

Write a decimal that matches each base ten block group.

29.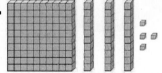

30.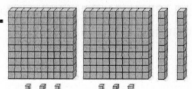

31.

Write each decimal in word form.

32. 2.1

33. 70.07

34. 3.012

Find the area of each polygon.

35.
$2\frac{1}{4}$ in

36.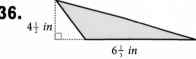
$4\frac{1}{2}$ in
$6\frac{1}{3}$ in

37.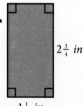
$2\frac{3}{4}$ in
$1\frac{1}{4}$ in

ORDERING AND COMPARING DECIMALS

 Order and compare decimals to find the smallest or largest decimal.

The ladies' short program for ice skating at the 2006 Olympic Winter Games in Torino ended with the following results:

Ice Skater	Total Segment Score
Irina Slutskaya	66.7
Shizuka Arakawa	66.02
Sasha Cohen	66.73

Source: http://www.torino2006.org

Comparing decimals is similar to comparing whole numbers.

Decimals that do not have the same number of digits after the decimal point can be compared by inserting zeros to hold place value. Decimals that name the same amount are called **equivalent decimals**.

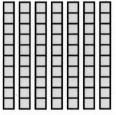

0.7 (seven tenths) = 0.70 (seventy hundredths)

EXAMPLE 1

Use place value to list the scores of Irina Slutskaya (66.7), Shizuka Arakawa (66.02) and Sasha Cohen (66.73) from greatest to least.

SOLUTION

Line up the decimal points.

66.70 — Irina Slutskaya's score of 66.7 = 66.70
66.02
66.73 — Insert a zero to hold place value.

Starting from the left and moving right, compare the digits until there is a digit that differs.

The tenths place is different.

Compare the digits in the tenths place.

0 < 7 so 66.02 is the smallest.

Compare the digits in the hundredths place for the two remaining numbers.

66.70
66.73
0 < 3 so 66.70 < 66.73

Sasha had the highest score (66.73). Irina had the next highest score (66.7). Shizuka had the lowest score (66.02) of the three figure skaters.

EXAMPLE 2

Use a number line to compare 7.4 and 7.38.

Decimals on a number line get larger as you move from left to right.

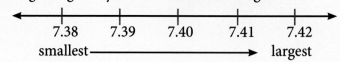

Put the decimals on a number line.

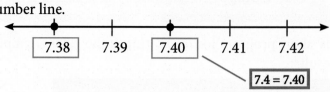

7.38 < 7.4

EXAMPLE 3

Put the following numbers in order from least to greatest.
12,   12.11,   12.01,   12.113

Line up the decimal points. Insert zeros
so each number has the same number
of places after the decimal point.

12.000
12.110
12.010
12.113

Use place value to compare digits.

The order from least to greatest is: 12, 12.01, 12.11, 12.113

EXPLORE!   **BATTING AVERAGES**

PLAYER	BATTING AVERAGE
Lin	0.15
Jacie	0.187
Sorrell	0.300
Libby	0.143
Octavia	0.24
Jaelynn	0.14
Maria	0.2
Leslie	0.198
Julia	0.31
Thora	0.185
Kate	0.141
Brynn	0.240
Sarah	0.252
Isabelle	0.3

The Jackson Middle School Fastpitch coach kept track of the players' batting averages. At the end of the season, the batting averages were posted (see the table on the left). Batting averages are usually listed to the thousandths place. When the averages were posted, some were only listed to the tenths or hundredths place. Help the players figure out their batting averages. (Note: The larger the decimal, the better the batting average.)

Step 1: Who had the best batting average? How do you know?

Step 2: Who had the worst batting average? How do you know?

Step 3: Use >, < and = to compare batting averages.
   a. Jacie and Thora   **d.** Lin and Julia
   b. Isabelle and Sorrell   **e.** Kate and Jaelynn
   c. Octavia and Brynn   **f.** Jaelynn and Libby

EXPLORE!

Step 4: List each group from least to greatest according to their batting averages.
  a. Maria, Octavia, Leslie, Kate
  b. Lin, Jacie, Isabelle, Sarah, Jaelynn
  c. Brynn, Thora, Julia, Maria, Libby

Step 5: Put the whole team's batting averages in order from least to greatest.

EXERCISES

Replace each  with <, > or = to make a true sentence.

1. 3.1 ◯ 3.2

2. 7.03 ◯ 7.3

3. 5.751 ◯ 5.75

4. 6.5 ◯ 6.50

5. 42.9 ◯ 42.19

6. 4.567 ◯ 4.678

7. 2.140 ◯ 2.104

8. 32.7 ◯ 32.70

9. 1.11 ◯ 1.111

Put each set of numbers in order from least to greatest.

10. 4.45, 4.4, 4.44, 4.42

11. 17.801, 17.81, 17.8, 17.851

12. 5.9, 5.99, 5.09, 5.999

Circle the best answer for each question.

13. Which number is between 6.77 and 6.97?
  A. 6.7
  B. 6.98
  C. 6.9
  D. 6.07

14. Which number is larger than 2.421?
  A. 2.42
  B. 2.425
  C. 2.4
  D. 2.411

15. Which number is smaller than eight and eight hundred four thousandths?
  A. 8.9   **B.** 8.805   **C.** 8.84   **D.** 8.8

Nine different runners' times for the 400 meter dash are displayed in the table. Use the information in the table to complete the following problems.

400 *m* dash time (in seconds)
50.5
49.09
49.45
49.76
49.25
51.5
48.9
50.98
49.61

16. _____ is the fastest time.

17. _____ and _____ are slower than 50.55.

18. _____ is the slowest time.

19. _____ and _____ are faster than 49.2.

20. _____ and _____ are between 50.45 and 51.05.

21. _____ is equal to 49.760.

22. Put the times in order from least to greatest (fastest to slowest).

23. Ethan drank 2.2 liters of water on Friday and 2.25 liters of water on Saturday. On which day did he drink less water?

24. The temperature on Monday was 68.75° F. On Tuesday, it was 68.8° F. Wednesday's temperature was 68.08° F.
   a. Which day was the hottest?
   b. Which day was the coolest?
   c. Put the three temperatures in order from least to greatest.

Many states have a minimum wage law. The least amount an employer can pay an employee is this wage per hour. Use the 2007 Minimum Wage chart to answer each question.

State	Minimum Wage
Alaska	$7.15
Oregon	$7.80
Washington	$7.93
California	$7.50
Idaho	$5.85
Nevada	$6.33

http://www.dol.gov.miniwage/America.html

25. Which state has the highest minimum wage?

26. Which state has the lowest minimum wage?

27. Put the six states in order from lowest minimum wage to highest minimum wage.

REVIEW

Round each number to the underlined digit.

28. $\underline{4}$.507

29. 32.6$\underline{3}$4

30. 7.$\underline{9}$86

Write each number in word form as a decimal.

31. Two and seventeen hundredths **32.** Fifty and two thousandths **33.** Six and four tenths

ESTIMATING WITH DECIMALS

Estimate sums, differences, products or quotients of expressions involving decimals.

Klamath County could publish the following information:

There are 10,500 students in the county.
Klamath County has 28 public schools.

Which of the statements is an estimate?
Which is an exact statement?

There are situations where using an estimate makes sense. The number of students in Klamath County Schools probably changes every day because students move in and out of the county. The number of schools does not change often, so this is an exact statement.

Estimates are sometimes given instead of exact answers. It is confusing to say that the average American family has 2.4 children. Instead, it is often said that the average American family has about two children. The most common method for estimating decimal expressions is to round to the nearest whole number before calculating.

EXAMPLE 1	**The Oregon State bird, the Western Meadowlark, weighs between 3.18 and 5.3 ounces. Estimate the difference between the heaviest weight and the lightest weight given.**

SOLUTION

Use rounding to estimate the difference. $5.30 - 3.18$

Round each number to the $5.30 \rightarrow 5$ $3.18 \rightarrow 3$
nearest whole number.
Subtract. $5 - 3 = 2$ so $5.3 - 3.18 \approx 2$

The difference between the heaviest and lightest weight for the Western Meadowlark is about 2 ounces.

EXAMPLE 2	**Apples cost \$1.97 per pound. Ieysha buys a bag of apples that weighs 4.7 pounds. About how much money did Ieysha need to purchase the apples?**

SOLUTION

Use rounding to estimate the product. $\$1.97 \times 4.7$

Round each number to the $\$1.97 \rightarrow \$2$ $4.7 \rightarrow 5$
nearest whole number.
Multiply. $\$2 \times 5 = \$10$ so $\$1.97 \times 4.7 \approx \$10$

Ieysha needed about \$10.00 to purchase the apples.

Compatible numbers can be used when estimating quotients. Round the divisor to the nearest whole number. Change the dividend to the nearest multiple of the new divisor. This makes the two numbers compatible, or easy to compute mentally.

EXAMPLE 3

Maris saved $121.28 to buy board games for her nieces and nephews. The board games she bought cost $19.95 each. Approximately how many board games did she buy?

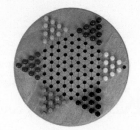

SOLUTION

Use compatible numbers to estimate. $121.28 ÷ $19.95

Round the divisor to the nearest whole number. $121.28 ÷ $20

Change the dividend to the nearest multiple of the new divisor. $120 ÷ $20 = 6

Maris bought about six board games.

EXERCISES

Use rounding to the nearest whole number to estimate each sum or difference.

1. 4.6 + 2.9

2. 5.678 + 1.231

3. 7.9 + 5.21

4. 2.12 − 1.04

5. 9.61 − 3.3

6. 12.99 − 4.6

7. 8.73 + 8.29 + 8.9

8. 11.051 + 12.523 + 2.423

9. 15.4 + 4.8 + 2.4

10. Zade is the cashier for his family's garage sale. A lady wants to buy a bag of clothes for $5.75 plus a few books for $5.40. Approximately how much money will she owe Zade?

11. Xavier took $33.25 to the store. He bought a CD that cost $17.85. About how much money did he have left?

Use rounding to the nearest whole number to estimate each product.

12. 6.22 × 3.54

13. 3.98 × 4.123

14. 9.84 × 4.89

15. 9.04 × 3.13

16. 19.941 × 4.784

17. 36.05 × 6.322

18. Jessica buys 3.4 pounds of bulk candy. It costs $1.78 per pound. Approximately how much will the candy cost Jessica?

19. Jorgé earned $10.60 per hour for 19.25 hours of work. About how much did he earn?

Use compatible numbers to estimate each quotient.

20. $123.4 \div 24.95$

21. $33.567 \div 7.05$

22. $93.3 \div 9.05$

23. $30.901 \div 11.167$

24. $51.33 \div 2.211$

25. $19.275 \div 21.01$

26. Stefani orders 8.8 yards of fabric. It takes 2.5 yards of fabric for each of her projects. Estimate how many projects Stefani can sew with the fabric she ordered.

27. Mya went to the bookstore to buy books for herself. She had $59.15 to spend. Each book she bought cost $5.95. About how many books did she buy?

REVIEW

Replace each ⬤ with <, > or = to make a true sentence.

28. 2.8 ⬤ 2.85

29. 7.010 ⬤ 7.01

30. 6.755 ⬤ 6.76

Put each group of numbers in order from least to greatest.

31. 32.4, 32.43, 32.34, 32.48

32. 17.9, 18, 17.09, 18.9

33. 11.02, 11.22, 11.022, 11.2

Find each sum, difference, product or quotient.

34. $2\frac{1}{2} \times 1\frac{3}{4}$

35. $5\frac{1}{4} \div 3\frac{1}{2}$

36. $1\frac{7}{8} + 1\frac{3}{4}$

37. $6\frac{1}{5} - 2\frac{1}{10}$

38. $3\frac{1}{6} \div 7\frac{5}{6}$

39. $4\frac{2}{3} \times 5\frac{1}{2}$

TIC-TAC-TOE ~ PLACE VALUE STORY

Fiction picture books contain short stories that have a problem and a solution. Write your own fiction story about place value with decimals as your characters. Their problem is that they can not figure out which one of them is the largest. A complete fiction picture book will include illustrations, a cover and a title.

ADDING AND SUBTRACTING DECIMALS

LESSON 25

 Find sums or differences of expressions involving decimals.

Laura walked one mile or 1,609.344 meters on Friday. She walked three-quarters of a mile or 1,207.008 meters on Saturday. She wants to keep track of her total meters walked. She will need to add these decimals together.

ADDING OR SUBTRACTING DECIMALS

1. Line up the decimal points.
2. Insert zeros so each decimal has the same amount of places after the decimal point.
3. Add or subtract.
4. Move the decimal point down into the answer in its same position.

EXAMPLE 1 Laura walked 1,609.344 meters on Friday and 1,207.008 meters on Saturday. How many meters did she walk altogether?

SOLUTION

Write the problem. $1609.344 + 1207.008$

Line up the decimal points.
$$\begin{array}{r} 1609.344 \\ +\ 1207.008 \\ \hline \end{array}$$

Add.
$$\begin{array}{r} \overset{1}{1}60\overset{1}{9}.344 \\ +\ 1207.008 \\ \hline 2816.352 \end{array}$$

Laura walked 2,816.352 meters altogether.

EXAMPLE 2 Laura walked 1,628.3 meters on Sunday and 1,207.25 meters on Monday. How many more meters did Laura walk on Sunday than on Monday?

SOLUTION

Write the problem. $1628.3 - 1207.25$

Line up the decimal points.
$$\begin{array}{r} 1628.3 \\ -\ 1207.25 \\ \hline \end{array}$$

> Zeros can be added at the end of a decimal without changing the value of the number.

Insert zeros.
$$\begin{array}{r} 1628.30 \\ -\ 1207.25 \\ \hline \end{array}$$

Subtract.
$$\begin{array}{r} 1628.\overset{2\ 10}{\cancel{30}} \\ -\ 1207.25 \\ \hline 421.05 \end{array}$$

On Sunday, Laura walked 421.05 meters more than on Monday.

Many Americans are not exercising enough according to a study published in 2007 by the American Council of Exercise. The table below shows the results from a study documenting how many steps (and the conversion of steps to miles) were taken by people in different occupations.

The average total distance in miles is shown in the last column. For example, the secretaries in this study walked, on average, 1.7 ± .66 miles each day. This means:

Shortest Distance	Longest Distance
1.7 − .66	1.7 + .66
$\overset{6\ 10}{1.\cancel{70}}$	$\overset{1}{1.70}$
− .66	+ .66
1.04	2.36

Table 1. Average steps and distance walked by people in different occupations over the course of an average working day.		
Occupation	**Total Steps**	**Total Distance (mi)**
Secretaries	4,327 ± 1,671	1.7 ± .66
Teachers	4,726 ± 1,832	1.9 ± .73
Lawyers	5,062 ± 1,837	2.0 ± .73
Police officers	5,336 ± 1,767	2.1 ± .70
Nurses	8,648 ± 2,461	3.4 ± .98[a]
Construction workers	9,646 ± 2,719	3.8 ± 1.08[a]
Factory workers	9,892 ± 2,496	3.9 ± .99[a]
Restaurant servers	10,087 ± 2,908	4.0 ± 1.15[a]
Custodians	12,991 ± 4,902	5.2 ± 1.94[a,b]
Mail carriers	18,904 ± 5,624	7.5 ± 2.23[a,b,c]

[a]Significantly different than secretaries, teachers, lawyers and police officers ($p<.05$).

[b]Significantly different than nurses, construction workers, factory workers and restaurant servers ($p<.05$).

[c]Significantly different than all other occupations ($p<.05$).

Source: http://www.acefitness.org

Use the table to answer the following questions.

Step 1: What was the longest average total distance walked each day by:
   a. nurses?
   b. restaurant servers?
   c. mail carriers?

Step 2: What was the shortest average total distance walked each day by:
   a. construction workers?
   b. lawyers?
   c. mail carriers?

Step 3: Use the first number of each expression in the total distance column to determine how much further on average _____ walked each day than _____ .
   a. mail carriers, secretaries?
   b. construction workers, teachers?
   c. restaurant servers, police officers?

Example: custodians and nurses
Custodians' 1ˢᵗ number: 5.2 ± 1.94
Nurses' 1ˢᵗ number: 3.4 ± .98

$$\overset{4\ 12}{5.\cancel{2}}$$
$$- 3.4$$
$$1.8$$

Custodians walked, on average, 1.8 miles more than nurses.

EXERCISES

Find each sum.

1. 2.1 + 3.4

2. 4.32 + 5.29

3. 3.786 + 9.42

4. 4.607 + 3.4

5. 1.325 + 5.78

6. 53.999 + 32.187

7. Monica spent $15.17 on a pair of pants and $4.96 on a pair of socks. How much did she spend altogether?

Find each difference.

8. 7.2 – 2.5

9. 4.31 – 1.75

10. 8.241 – 6.456

11. 12.1 – 9.24

12. 6.087 – 3.43

13. 15.55 – 11.901

14. Chan filled his car with 12.85 gallons of gas one week. The next week he filled his car with 9.08 gallons. How any more gallons of gas did he put in his car the first week than the second week?

The table at the right shows the monthly rainfall in Florence, Oregon, for 2005. Use the table to answer each question.

Month	Rainfall (inches)
January	8.07
February	2.85
March	6.22
April	5.02
May	5.86
June	3.31
July	1
August	0.03
September	2.72
October	5.59
November	8.44
December	15.58

Source: http://www.trhunter.com/

15. How many inches of rain fell in Florence in September and October altogether?

16. How many more inches of rainfall did Florence have in November than in October?

17. How many more inches of rainfall did Florence have in December than in March?

18. How many inches of rainfall did Florence have in May and June altogether?

19. How many total inches of rainfall did Florence accumulate in February, March and April?

20. How many total inches of rainfall did Florence have in the last two months of the year?

21. What was the total rainfall in Florence during the first two months of the year?

22. Describe the process of adding two decimals.

23. Nachelle had $271.74 in her checking account. She wrote two checks. One was for $52.49 and the other was for $14.88. How much money did she have left in her checking account?

REVIEW

24. Write a decimal that would be between 1.5 and 2.

25. Write a decimal that is bigger than 3.4 but smaller than 3.5.

26. Write a decimal that is smaller than 5.056 but bigger than 5.05.

27. Round 4.678 to the nearest hundredth.

28. Round 23.969 to the nearest tenth.

29. Round 4.3809 to the nearest thousandth.

Find the value of each expression. Write in simplest form.

30. $\dfrac{3}{4} + \dfrac{1}{8}$

31. $2\frac{1}{2} \times 1\frac{1}{2}$

32. $\dfrac{7}{10} - \dfrac{7}{20}$

33. $3\frac{2}{3} + 1\frac{4}{5}$

34. $\dfrac{14}{39} \div \dfrac{2}{13}$

35. $2\frac{2}{5} \div 1\frac{1}{2}$

TIC-TAC-TOE ~ CHECKBOOK REGISTRY

You received $300 to spend on gifts for family and friends. Create a checkbook registry like the one below. Write $300.00 as your first deposit entry.

Use local advertisements to cut out items you would like to buy. Write each item and its price into the registry. Subtract the price from the running total.

Example:

Original Deposit		+$300.00
Shoes	$49.96	−$49.96
		$250.04
Portable DVD Player	$89.99	−$89.99
		$160.05
Curling Iron	$10.99	−$10.99
		$149.06
MP3 Player	$79.99	−$79.99
		$69.07
Digital Frame	$68.99	−$68.99
		$0.08

RULES: You must "buy" at least five gifts. (You do not really have to buy them.)
You must purchase gifts until you have less than one dollar left.

Create a poster with copies of the advertised prices of the gifts you "purchased" and a copy of your checkbook registry.

MULTIPLYING DECIMALS

LESSON 26

Find products of expressions involving decimals.

Yana had make-your-own banana splits for her birthday party. She had toppings at home, but she purchased three half-gallons of ice cream and 3.6 pounds of bananas. How much did these items cost?

Ice cream: $3.55 per half gallon	Bananas: $0.40 per pound

MULTIPLYING WITH DECIMALS

1. Multiply as if the numbers were whole numbers.
2. Count the number of places after the decimal points in each factor.
3. Count the same number of places in the product starting from the right and moving left.
4. Insert zeros, if needed, to hold place value. Delete zeros that are not necessary.
5. Put the decimal point where you stop counting in the answer.

EXAMPLE 1

How much did Yana spend on three half-gallons of ice cream if each half-gallon cost $3.55?

SOLUTION

Write the problem. $3 \times \$3.55$

Use decimal models to visualize.

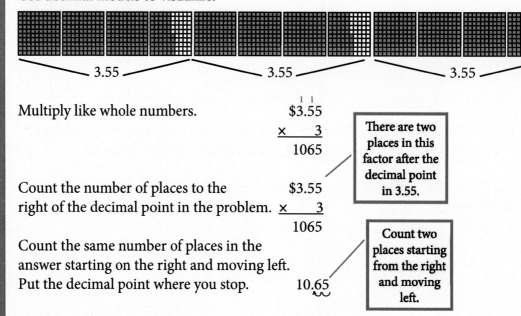

3.55   3.55   3.55

Multiply like whole numbers.

$$\begin{array}{r} \overset{1\ 1}{\$3.55} \\ \times \quad 3 \\ \hline 1065 \end{array}$$

There are two places in this factor after the decimal point in 3.55.

Count the number of places to the right of the decimal point in the problem.

$$\begin{array}{r} \$3.55 \\ \times \quad 3 \\ \hline 1065 \end{array}$$

Count the same number of places in the answer starting on the right and moving left. Put the decimal point where you stop.

Count two places starting from the right and moving left.

10.65

Yana spent $10.65 on ice cream.

EXAMPLE 2

SOLUTION

How much did Yana spend on 3.6 pounds of bananas. They cost $0.40 per pound?

Write the problem.   3.6 × $0.40 =

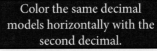

Color decimal models vertically to match the first decimal.

Color the same decimal models horizontally with the second decimal.

Where the two colors overlap is the answer.

Use decimal models to visualize.

3.6

0.40

0.4 + 0.4 + 0.4 + 0.24 = 1.44

Multiply like whole numbers.

$$\begin{array}{r} \overset{2}{3.6} \\ \times\ 0.40 \\ \hline 00 \\ +\ 1440 \\ \hline 1440 \end{array}$$

There is one place after the decimal point in the factor 3.6.

There are two places after the decimal point in the factor 0.40.

Count the number of digits to the right of the decimal points in both numbers in the problem.

$$\begin{array}{r} 3.6 \\ \times\ 0.40 \\ \hline 1440 \end{array}$$

Count three places starting from the right and moving left.

Count the same number of places in the answer starting on the right and moving left. Put the decimal point where you stop.   1.440

Drop any zeros at the end of the decimal.   1.440 = 1.44

Yana spent $1.44 on bananas.

EXAMPLE 3

SOLUTION

Find the value of 0.3 × 0.016.

Multiply like whole numbers.

$$\begin{array}{r} 0.016 \\ \times\ 0.3 \\ \hline 48 \end{array}$$

Count the number of digits to the right of the decimal points in both numbers in the problem.

$$\begin{array}{r} 0.016 \\ \times\ 0.3 \\ \hline 48 \end{array}$$

There are three places after the decimal point in the factor 0.016.

There is one place after the decimal point in the factor 0.3.

Count the same number of places in the answer starting on the right and moving left. Insert zeros to hold the missing places. Put the decimal point where you stop.   .0048

Count four places starting from the right and moving left.

0.3 × 0.016 = 0.0048

Jay gets advertisements for the local grocery stores in his newspaper. He wants to save the most money possible. He figures out which stores he should buy which items from. Here is part of his list and the stores with sales on those items.

ABC Grocery
Grapes: $1.39 per pound
Cherry tomatoes: $0.98 per pound
Fuji apples: $1.29 per pound
Deli-sliced ham: $3.99 per pound
Chicken breasts: $1.69 per pound
Whole chicken fryer: $0.69 per pound
Beef round roast: $1.98 per pound
Chocolate Blitz bars: $0.59 each
Fizzy Pop: $0.70 each

ZYX Grocery
Grapes: 3 pound container for $4.99
Cherry tomatoes: 3.5 pound container $3.96
Fuji apples: 3.25 pound bag for $4.25
Deli-sliced ham: 1.75 pound package for $5.50
Chicken breasts: 4 pound bag for $5.99
Whole chicken fryer: $5.50 for 5 pounds
Beef round roast: 4.5 pound roast for $9.23
Chocolate Blitz bars: $6.40 for bag of 12
Fizzy Pop: $9.99 for 15 pack

From which store should Jay buy grapes?

Step 1: Multiply the price at ABC Grocery ($1.39) by the number of pounds he would buy if he bought grapes at ZYX Grocery (3 pounds).

Step 2: Round to the nearest penny or hundredth if the total price when multiplied ends with more than two places after the decimal point. This is the price for the same amount of grapes at ABC Grocery.

Step 3: Compare prices. Which store has the lower price?

Step 4: Use the procedure from **Steps 1-3** for each item. Decide which store has the best price for each item on Jay's list.

EXERCISES

Find each product.

1. 4.1 × 3

2. 5 × 3.33

3. 7 × $2.17

4. 6.312 × 4

5. $4.89 × 5

6. 6 × 9.765

7. Celia's cell phone company charges $0.39 per minute if she goes over her allotted minutes for the month. Last month she went over by 15 minutes. How much extra did she owe on her bill?

8. Kenyan bought three pairs of pants that were on sale for $12.99 per pair. How much did he pay altogether?

9. 3.2 × 7.4

10. 2.5 × 6.6

11. 12.3 × 2.8

12. 10.45 × 4.1

13. 5.72 × 3.4

14. 11.5 × 7.62

15. 0.5×0.9

16. 0.3×0.46

17. $\$0.35 \times 0.8$

18. Hakeem bought 4.2 pounds of almonds. They cost $2.45 per pound. How much did Hakeem pay for the almonds?

19. The price tag under the 11.5 ounce bag of chips at the grocery store says $0.24 per ounce. How much does the bag of chips cost?

20. 0.012×3

21. 2.1×0.025

22. 4.12×0.0065

REVIEW

List each set of numbers from least to greatest.

23. $\frac{1}{2}$, $\frac{2}{3}$, $\frac{5}{12}$

24. 0.6, 0.62, 0.58

25. 1.31, 1.089, 1.4

26. 0.1, 0.09, 0.05

27. $\frac{3}{10}$, $\frac{2}{5}$, $\frac{7}{20}$

28. $1\frac{1}{3}$, $1\frac{1}{2}$, $1\frac{5}{6}$

Find the area of each polygon.

29.

$2\frac{1}{4}$ *in*
$4\frac{1}{2}$ *in*

30.
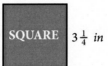
SQUARE $3\frac{1}{4}$ *in*

31.
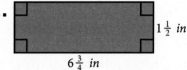
$1\frac{1}{2}$ *in*
$6\frac{3}{4}$ *in*

TIC-TAC-TOE ~ PURCHASE SPREADSHEET

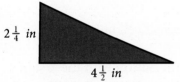

Step 1: Copy and complete the table below. For example, if your favorite movie is "What's Up," write that in the "My Favorite" column beside "Movie." Find the cost of each item at a store, on the internet or in a newspaper advertisement. Record the price in the "Price" column.

Step 2: Open a spreadsheet program on a computer. Create column headings for a chart as listed below.

      In cell A1 type: Category
      In cell B1 type: My Favorite
      In cell C1 type: Price
      In cell D1 type: Price for Three

Category	My Favorite	Price
Book		
DVD		
Board game		
Snack		
CD		
Video game		
Beverage		
Food		

Continued on next page

Step 3: Type the categories from **Step 1** in cells A2 through A9. You can adjust the width of the cell for category columns by placing your curser on the line between boxes A and B at the top of the spreadsheet. As the cursor touches the line, it becomes a "t" shape with arrows pointing in either direction. Click and drag the line to the right to make the cells for column A wider.

Step 4: Type the name of your favorite item in each category from **Step 1** in cells B2 through B9. Make the column wider following the procedure in **Step 3**.

Step 5: Enter the price for each item in the B column using a decimal point in cells C2 through C9.

> *Example:* Type "23.95" for a price that reads $23.95.

> *Hint:* To create cells displaying dollar amounts, highlight the cells which need a dollar sign, go to "Format" on the menu bar and select "cells." On the left hand list select "numbers" and choose "currency" from the list under the word "category."

Step 6: Type = "3*C2" in cell D2 and press the "enter" key. This tells the spreadsheet program to multiply the value in C2 by 3. As you type "C2" a blue box will highlight C2. Check the highlighted box to make sure you have selected the price you want to multiply by 3. After pressing "enter," a price should appear in D2 that is three times the amount of the price in C2. *Note:* In a spreadsheet, the * symbol represents multiplication.

Step 7: Continue the process in **Step 6** with the cells in column D. Use the correct cell number.

Step 8: When you have prices for three of each item, click on cell C10. Find the button with the Σ sign at the top of the spreadsheet. Click on the Σ and "=SUM(C2:C9)" will appear in cell C10. Press enter. This gives the total for all amounts in column C. Click on cell D10 then the Σ sign. The function "=SUM(D2:D9)" will appear in D10. Press enter. This gives the total for all amounts in column D.

Step 9: Highlight all cells with typing in them. Find the button at the top of the spreadsheet to create borders. Border all lines that are in the area you have highlighted. Print the spreadsheet by choosing "print selection" while the cells remain highlighted.

Step 10: Answer the following questions in complete sentences on a separate sheet of paper. Attach the answers to the spreadsheet.

> **1.** Which single item costs the most?
> **2.** If you buy three of your favorite books, one for yourself and two friends, how much would you spend?
> **3.** An advertisement has a coupon for "Buy three CDs, Get $4.99 Off." What would three CDs cost if you used the coupon?
> **4.** List the three cheapest items. What is the total cost if you buy three of each of these?
> **5.** List the four most expensive items. What is the total cost if you buy three of each of these?
> **6.** Many businesses and individuals budget their money with a spreadsheet. Why do you think they use spreadsheets?

DIVIDING DECIMALS BY WHOLE NUMBERS

Find quotients of expressions where decimals are divided by whole numbers.

Kainan's basketball coach purchased water bottles for him and his 11 teammates. The total cost was $4.80. The cost was divided equally among the players and coach. How much did Kainan owe?

When you have a full price and need to find out the unit price, you need to divide. Use base-ten blocks or money to visualize dividing decimals.

To find out how much Kainan owed for his water bottle, he divided $4.80 by 12.

Set out ones and tenths base-ten blocks or dollars and dimes to represent 4.80.

OR

Break the ones into tenths or the dollars into dimes.

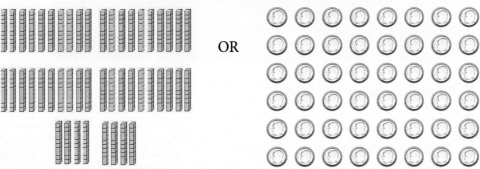

OR

Divide the tenths blocks or dimes into 12 groups.

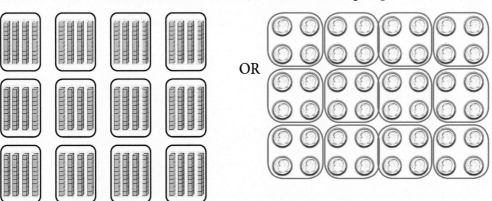

OR

How many tenths or dimes are in each group? There are 4 tenths or 0.4 or $0.40.
Kainan owes $0.40 for his water bottle.

EXAMPLE 1

Kassim bought 3.9 pounds of candy corn for a harvest party. He divided it among himself and nine friends. How many pounds of candy corn did each person get?

SOLUTION

Write the problem.

$$3.9 \div 10$$

Divide as if the divisor and dividend were whole numbers.

$$\begin{array}{r} 39 \\ 10\overline{)3.90} \\ -30 \\ \hline 90 \\ -90 \\ \hline 0 \end{array}$$

Insert a zero on the end of the dividend. Continue dividing.

When subtracting these numbers ignore the decimal point.

Move the decimal point into the quotient directly above the decimal point in the dividend.

$$\begin{array}{r} .39 \\ 10\overline{)3.90} \end{array}$$

Each person received 0.39 pounds of candy corn.

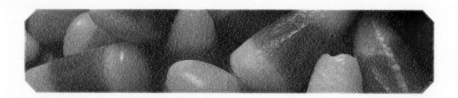

EXAMPLE 2

Find the value of 2.97 ÷ 30.

SOLUTION

Divide as if the divisor and dividend were whole numbers.

$$\begin{array}{r} 99 \\ 30\overline{)2.970} \\ -270 \\ \hline 270 \\ -270 \\ \hline 0 \end{array}$$

Insert a zero on the end of the dividend. Continue dividing.

Move the decimal point into the quotient directly above the decimal point in the dividend.

$$\begin{array}{r} . \_99 \\ 30\overline{)2.970} \end{array}$$

Insert a zero to hold the tenths place.

$$.099$$

$$2.97 \div 30 = 0.099$$

Sometimes there is a remainder when dividing decimals. Round to a designated place-value when that happens. Divide until the quotient has one more place-value position than where it is being rounded to. This helps you know whether to round up or down.

EXAMPLE 3

Janease spent $3.22 to download three songs. Each song cost about the same amount. How much did she spend on each song? Round to the nearest penny (hundredth) if necessary.

SOLUTION

Write the problem

$$3.22 \div 3$$

Divide as if the divisor and dividend were whole numbers.

```
      1073 R1
  3)3.220
   -3
    02
   -00
    22
   -21
    10
    -9
     1
```

Insert a zero on the end of the dividend and continue dividing.

Move the decimal point into the quotient directly above the decimal point in the dividend.

```
    1.073
  3)3.220
```

Round to the nearest penny.

1.07

Janease spent about $1.07 on each song.

EXAMPLE 4

Find the value of 16 ÷ 5.

SOLUTION

Place a decimal point in the dividend at the end of the whole number.

```
  5)16.
```

Divide.

```
     32
  5)16.0
   -15
    10
   -10
     0
```

Move the decimal into the quotient.

```
    3.2
  5)16.
```

$16 \div 5 = 3.2$

EXERCISES

Find each quotient.

1. 3.8 ÷ 2

2. $21.30 ÷ 3

3. 36.5 ÷ 5

4. $15.36 ÷ 6

5. 11.2 ÷ 4

6. 14.32 ÷ 8

7. The grocer charged Tory $4.47 for grapes. She bought three pounds of grapes. How much did each pound of grapes cost?

8. Carole bought six bouquets of flowers. Each bouquet cost the same amount. She spent a total of $59.88. How much did each bouquet cost?

9. Vashti was paid for every weed she pulled. She pulled 25 weeds. She earned $3.00. How much was she paid for each weed?

10. 0.63 ÷ 7

11. 1.05 ÷ 12

12. 0.97 ÷ 10

13. 1.47 ÷ 15

14. 1.68 ÷ 21

15. 4.6 ÷ 4

16. There were 0.5 gallons of milk in the refrigerator for a family of eight. Each person drank the same amount of milk. How much of a gallon did each person drink?

17. Twelve people split $18.00 equally. How much money did each person receive?

Find each quotient. Round your answer to the nearest hundredth.

18. $13.42 ÷ 6

19. 8.7 ÷ 7

20. 41 ÷ 7

21. 11.9 ÷ 3

22. $50.63 ÷ 5

23. 21.493 ÷ 4

Store	Weight in pounds	Total Price
Alan's	4	$6.60
Food Market	2	$3.55
Save More	3	$5.10

24. The table gives information for purchasing dried apricots at three different grocery stores.
　　a. Find the price per pound at each store. Round to the nearest penny.
　　b. Which store has the best buy?

REVIEW

25. Estimate each sum or difference.
　　a. 14.24 − 4.52
　　b. 4.224 + 4.24

26. Find each sum or difference
　　a. 14.24 − 4.52
　　b. 4.224 + 4.24

27. Estimate each product.
　　a. $4\frac{1}{5} \times 2\frac{1}{3}$
　　b. $10\frac{3}{4} \times 1\frac{1}{10}$

28. Find each product.
　　a. $4\frac{1}{5} \times 2\frac{1}{3}$
　　b. $10\frac{3}{4} \times 1\frac{1}{10}$

Find quotients of expressions where decimals are divided by decimals.

Dividing requires you to look at how many groups of one number fit into another number. When dividing decimals, the same approach applies.

24 ÷ 6 can be read as, "How many groups of 6 fit in the number 24?"

2.4 ÷ 0.6 can be read as, "How many groups of 0.6 fit in the number 2.4?"

Base-ten blocks can be used to model 2.4 ÷ 6.

Set out base-ten blocks to model the dividend, 2.4.

Substitute any ones blocks with tenths because the divisor is tenths.

Move the tenths into groups the size of the divisor.

There are 4 groups of 0.6 in 2.4. $2.4 \div 0.6 = 4$

This means that 2.4 is four times greater than 0.6. $0.6 \times 4 = 2.4$

DIVIDING DECIMALS BY DECIMALS

1. Change the divisor into a whole number by moving the decimal point to the right.
2. Move the decimal point in the dividend the same number of places to the right as it was moved in the divisor.
3. Divide the dividend by the divisor.
4. Move the decimal point into the quotient directly above the decimal point in the dividend.
5. Insert zeros, if necessary, to hold place values.

EXAMPLE 1

SOLUTION

Thuyet purchased 3.2 pounds of fertilizer for $4.48. To determine how much he paid per pound you must find $4.48 \div 3.2$.

Rewrite the problem. When dividing by a decimal the divisor needs to be a whole number. Do this by moving the decimal point to the right in the divisor first.

Divisor

3.2.

The decimal point in the dividend must be moved the same number of places to the right as in the divisor.

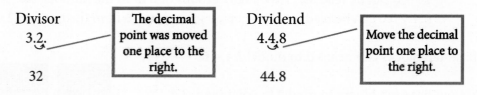

Divisor	The decimal point was moved one place to the right.	Dividend	Move the decimal point one place to the right.
3.2.		4.4.8	
32		44.8	

Find the quotient using the new dividend and divisor.

$$44.8 \div 32$$

$$\begin{array}{r} 1.4 \\ 32\overline{)44.8} \\ \underline{-32} \\ 128 \\ \underline{-128} \\ 0 \end{array}$$

$$44.8 \div 32 = 1.4 \;\rightarrow\; 4.48 \div 3.2 = 1.4$$

Thuyet's fertilizer cost $1.40 per pound.

EXAMPLE 2

SOLUTION

Find the value of $67.2 \div 0.56$.

Change the divisor into a whole number and move the decimal point the same number of places to the right in both divisor and the dividend.

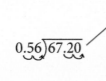

> Insert a zero on the end of the dividend to hold place-value when the decimal point is moved.

Divide the dividend by the divisor as if both were whole numbers.

$$\begin{array}{r} 120 \\ 56\overline{)6720} \\ \underline{-56} \\ 112 \\ \underline{-112} \\ 00 \end{array}$$

> Zero is the last digit in the quotient because $0 \div 56 = 0$

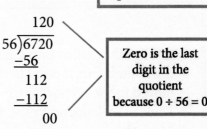

Move the decimal point into the quotient directly above the decimal point in the dividend.

$$\begin{array}{r} 120. \\ 56\overline{)6720.} \end{array}$$

$$67.2 \div 0.56 = 120$$

EXAMPLE 3

Joe makes $8.30 per hour. Macie makes $12.45 per hour. How many times greater is Macie's hourly pay than Joe's hourly pay?

SOLUTION

To find how many times greater Macie's hourly pay is, write a multiplication equation.

$8.30 × _____ = $12.45

Use division to find the missing number.

$12.45 ÷ $8.30

Change the divisor into a whole number. Move the decimal point the same number of places to the right in both the divisor and the dividend.

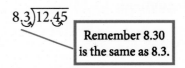

> Remember 8.30 is the same as 8.3.

Divide the dividend by the divisor as if both were whole numbers.

$$\begin{array}{r} 15 \\ 83\overline{)124.5} \\ -83 \\ \hline 415 \\ -415 \\ \hline 0 \end{array}$$

Move the decimal point into the quotient directly above the decimal point in the dividend.

$$\begin{array}{r} 1.5 \\ 83\overline{)124.5} \end{array}$$

Macie makes 1.5 times the amount per hour that Joe makes.

EXAMPLE 4

Annette put 10.912 gallons of gas into her car last week. This week she put in 10.02 gallons of gas. How many times greater was the amount of gasoline last week than this week? Round to the nearest tenth.

SOLUTION

Change the divisor into a whole number. Move the decimal point the same number of places to the right in both divisor and the dividend.

$$10.02\overline{)10.912}$$

Divide the dividend by the divisor as if both were whole numbers.

$$\begin{array}{r} 108 \\ 1002\overline{)1091.20} \\ -1002 \\ \hline 892 \\ -0 \\ \hline 8920 \\ -8016 \\ \hline 904 \end{array}$$

> Stop dividing when you have one more place-value position in the quotient than needed.

Move the decimal point into the quotient directly above the decimal point in the dividend.

$$\begin{array}{r} 1.08 \\ 1002\overline{)1091.20} \end{array}$$

Round to the nearest tenth.

$1.08 ≈ 1.1$

Last week's fill-up was 1.1 times more than this week's fill-up.

EXERCISES

Rewrite each division problem so the divisor is a whole number.

1. 4.8 ÷ 0.8

2. 10.28 ÷ 2.55

3. 124 ÷ 3.4

4. 10.85 ÷ 7.75

5. 18.29 ÷ 3.1

6. 9.9 ÷ 6.62

Find each quotient.

7. 2.7 ÷ 0.3

8. 4.8 ÷ 3.2

9. 4.9 ÷ 0.07

10. 9.72 ÷ 5.4

11. 14 ÷ 0.4

12. 0.115 ÷ 0.025

13. 32.8 ÷ 0.5

14. 7.1 ÷ 2.84

15. 4.42 ÷ 2.6

16. Susan spent $71.50 at the mall. Elise spent $28.60. How many times greater was Susan's spending than Elise's spending?

17. Sean's pumpkin weighed 33.12 pounds. Kevin's pumpkin weighed 9.6 pounds. How many times heavier was Sean's pumpkin than Kevin's pumpkin?

Find each quotient. Round to the nearest tenth, if necessary.

18. 12.9 ÷ 4.6

19. 11.8 ÷ 2.7

20. 1.287 ÷ 0.25

21. 15.95 ÷ 3.95

22. 21.90 ÷ 6.89

23. 10.1 ÷ 1.01

24. The state of Oregon had an approximate population of 3.7 million people in 2006. The state of Washington had an approximate population of 6.4 million people in the same year. How many times greater was the population of Washington than the population of Oregon?

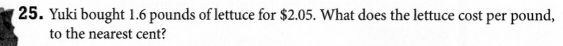
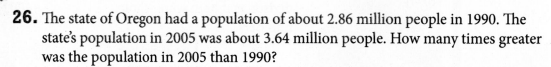

25. Yuki bought 1.6 pounds of lettuce for $2.05. What does the lettuce cost per pound, to the nearest cent?

26. The state of Oregon had a population of about 2.86 million people in 1990. The state's population in 2005 was about 3.64 million people. How many times greater was the population in 2005 than 1990?

27. Sharla weighs 52.4 kilograms. Troy weighs 83.84 kilograms. Troy's weight is how many times greater than Sharla's weight?

Find each product. Round to the nearest hundredth, if necessary.

28. 3.1 × 3.1

29. 9.52 × 4.5

30. 10.7 × 5.39

31. 2.8 × 0.072

32. 0.18 × 1.5

33. 15.1 × 0.48

TIC-TAC-TOE ~ DECIMAL POETRY

Ideas and thoughts can be expressed in poetry as a written form of art. Choose two different forms of poetry. Write one poem about multiplying decimals by decimals. Write another poem about dividing decimals by decimals.

Nonet

A nonet is a poem that consists of nine lines. Rhyming is optional. The first line has 9 syllables, the second line has 8 syllables. Continue through the ninth line which has only one syllable.

Free Verse

Free Verse is poetry that doesn't follow traditional poetry rules (meter and rhyme). Line breaks are used to create meaning and allow the reader to slow down, stop or speed up their reading to accentuate a part of the poem.

Song

A song is a rhythmic poem that has verses and a chorus. The chorus is repeated between each verse.

MEASURING IN CENTIMETERS

Measure and draw line segments using centimeters.

The **metric system** is used in a majority of countries around the world. The metric system is a decimal system of measurement. The basic unit of length in the metric system is the meter. Other metric units, such as millimeters, centimeters and kilometers, are based on the meter.

The United States is one of only a few countries that use the customary system as its primary system of measurement. Customary units of length include inches, feet, yards and miles.

There are many reasons you should learn about the metric system. When you purchase items made in other countries the measurements are often in metric units. You may travel in other countries where you need to read signs in metric units. Can you think of other situations where you might see measurements in metric units?

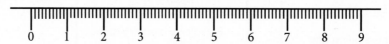

Each whole number on a metric ruler represents a centimeter (*cm*). The small tick marks between each centimeter represent millimeters (*mm*). There are 10 millimeters in 1 centimeter. Each millimeter is one-tenth of a centimeter.

EXAMPLE 1	**Find the length of the line to the nearest tenth of a centimeter.**

SOLUTION

Line the 0 mark on the ruler with the left edge of the line. Identify the tick mark that represents the length of the line.

Each small tick mark represents 0.1 centimeters. Count the number of tick marks after the last whole number to find the number of tenths.

6	+	0.3	=	6.3 *cm*
WHOLE NUMBER	+	TENTHS	=	TOTAL LENGTH

The length of the line is 6.3 *cm*.

Step 1: Use your ruler to measure the length of each object below to the nearest tenth of a centimeter. Record your answers.

Step 2: Sometimes measurements are approximated to the nearest half centimeter.
- **a.** Round each of the measurements from **Step 1** to the nearest half centimeter.
- **b.** What two decimal numbers can the measurements end with if they are rounded to the nearest half centimeter?

Step 3: Draw a line that fits each description.
- **a.** exactly 3.6 centimeters long
- **b.** exactly 0.8 centimeters long
- **c.** approximately 7 centimeters long

- **d.** exactly 7 centimeters long
- **e.** approximately 3.5 centimeters long
- **f.** approximately 1.5 centimeters long

Step 4: Are the lines from **part c and d** in **Step 3** the exact same length? Do they have to be? Why or why not?

Step 5: Estimate how long your pencil is in centimeters. Record your estimate. Measure your pencil to see how long it is. How far off was your estimate to the nearest tenth of a centimeter?

Step 6: Estimate the length (in centimeters) of two other objects in your classroom. Measure the objects to the nearest half centimeter. Approximately how far off were your estimates?

EXAMPLE 2   **Find the length of the line to the nearest half centimeter.**

SOLUTION   Line the 0 mark on the ruler with the left edge of the line. Identify the tick mark that represents the length of the line.

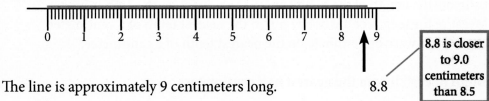

8.8 is closer to 9.0 centimeters than 8.5

The line is approximately 9 centimeters long.   8.8

EXERCISES

1. How many spaces is each centimeter divided into by the tick marks?

2. Round 3.2 to the nearest half centimeter.

3. Round 4.8 to the nearest half centimeter.

4. A line measured 3 centimeters and 4 millimeters. Write this measurement as a decimal with centimeter units.

5. A pen measured 14 centimeters and 1 millimeter. Write this measurement as a decimal with centimeter units.

Find the length of each line to the nearest tenth of a centimeter.

6. ━━━━━━━━━━━━━━━━━

7. ━━━━━━━━━━━━━━

8. ━━━━━━━━━━━━━━━━━━━━━━━

9. ━━━━━━━━━━━━━━━━━━━━

10. ━━━

11. ━━━━━━━

12. Use the pocket watch to the right.
   a. Estimate the width of the pocket watch to the nearest tenth of a centimeter.
   b. Measure the width of the pocket watch to the nearest tenth of a centimeter.
   c. How far off was your estimate, to the nearest tenth of a centimeter?

13. Use the bobby pin below.

   a. Estimate the length of the bobby pin to the nearest tenth of a centimeter.
   b. Measure the length of the bobby pin to the nearest tenth of a centimeter.
   c. How far off was your estimate, to the nearest tenth of a centimeter?

Find the length of each line to the nearest half centimeter.

14. ━━━━━━━━━━━━━━━

15. ━━━━━━━━━━━━━

16. _____

17. _____

18. _____

19. Use the key.

    a. Estimate the length of the key to the nearest half centimeter.
    b. Measure the length of the key to the nearest half centimeter.
    c. How far off was your estimate, to the nearest half centimeter?

20. Use the lemon.

    a. Estimate the length of the lemon to the nearest half centimeter.
    b. Measure the length of the length to the nearest half centimeter.
    c. How far off was your estimate, to the nearest half centimeter?

Draw a line with each given length.

21. 3.4 *cm*   **22.** 4.2 *cm*   **23.** 5.7 *cm*

24. 9.5 *cm*   **25.** 0.9 *cm*   **26.** 8 *cm*

27. Sammi needs to cut a sheet of metal into 4 equal pieces to complete her art project. The sheet of metal is 60.8 *cm* long. How long will each piece be?

28. Dave chose three lengths of cardboard to make a sign. The sign needs to measure 1 meter (100 *cm*) long. The three lengths of cardboard are 36.2 *cm*, 51.6 *cm*, and 11.2 *cm*. Will he have enough cardboard to make the sign?

REVIEW

Find each product or quotient.

29. 5.2×3.95 **30.** $3.69 \div 3$ **31.** $5.68 \div 0.4$

32. 22.7×0.6 **33.** 40×3.9 **34.** $12 \div 0.08$

AREA AND PERIMETER WITH DECIMALS

Calculate the perimeter and area of squares, rectangles and triangles using the metric system.

Metric measurements are written as decimals. Finding perimeter and area of figures that have metric measurements involves adding and multiplying decimals.

Celine's family landscaped their new backyard. The yard is a rectangle 50.5 meters long and 28.2 meters wide. They put a fence around the entire perimeter of the yard. How much fencing did they need?

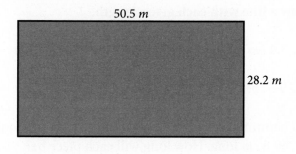

You must find the perimeter to find the distance around the yard. Remember that opposite sides of rectangles are equal in length.

Perimeter = length + width + length + width
Perimeter = 50.5 + 28.2 + 50.5 + 28.2

$$
\begin{array}{r}
50.5 \\
28.2 \\
50.5 \\
+\ 28.2 \\
\hline
157.4 \text{ meters}
\end{array}
$$

50.5 m
28.2 m

Celine's family also laid sod in the entire backyard. How many square meters of sod did they purchase?

To find out the amount of sod that will cover the backyard, you must find the area. The area of a rectangle is determined by multiplying the length times the width.

Area of a Rectangle = length × width
Area of Celine's Yard = 50.5 × 28.2

$$
\begin{array}{r}
50.5 \\
\times\ 28.2 \\
\hline
1010 \\
40400 \\
+\ 101000 \\
\hline
1424.10 \text{ square meters}
\end{array}
$$

Celine's family needed 157.4 meters of fencing and 1,424.1 square meters of sod for their backyard.

AREAS OF GEOMETRIC FIGURES

Rectangle: Area = length × width
Square: Area = side × side
Triangle: Area = $\frac{1}{2}$ × base × height *or* 0.5 × base × height

EXAMPLE 1

Measure the side lengths of the figure below in centimeters. Find the area.

SOLUTION

Measure the sides of the shape.

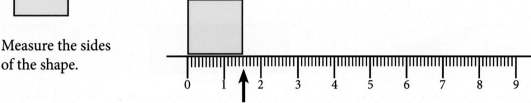

It is a square with 1.5 *cm* sides.

Square: Area = *side* × *side*   Area = 1.5 × 1.5

Multiply.

$$
\begin{array}{r}
1.5 \\
\times\ 1.5 \\
\hline
75 \\
+\ 150 \\
\hline
2.25
\end{array}
$$

> There is one place after the decimal point in each of the decimals 1.5 for a total of 2 places in the solution.

The area of the square is 2.25 square centimeters or 2.25 *cm²*.

EXAMPLE 2

Use the given measurements to find the area of the triangle.

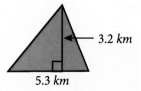
3.2 *km*
5.3 *km*

SOLUTION

The triangle area formula can be written two different ways.
$\frac{1}{2}$ × *base* × *height* or 0.5 × *base* × *height*
If the measurements are in decimals, use the formula that contains a decimal.

Area = 0.5 × *base* × *height*   Area = 0.5 × 5.3 × 3.2

Multiply the first two decimals.

$$
\begin{array}{r}
0.5 \\
\times\ 5.3 \\
\hline
15 \\
+\ 250 \\
\hline
265 \rightarrow 2.65
\end{array}
$$

> There is one place after the decimal point in each of the decimals 0.5 and 5.3 for a total of two places in the solution.

Multiply the answer from the first equation by the third number in the problem.

$$
\begin{array}{r}
2.65 \\
\times\ 3.2 \\
\hline
530 \\
+\ 7950 \\
\hline
8480 \rightarrow 8.48
\end{array}
$$

The area of the triangle is 8.48 square kilometers or 8.48 *km²*.

EXERCISES

Use the given measurements to find the perimeter and area of each figure.

1.
1.4 *cm*
5.5 *cm*

2.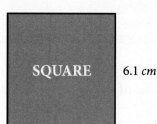
SQUARE
6.1 *cm*

3.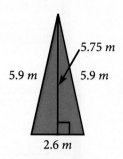
5.75 *m*
5.9 *m*   5.9 *m*
2.6 *m*

4.
6.9 km
4.9 km
3.2 km
4.9 km

5.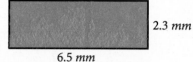
2.3 *mm*
6.5 *mm*

6.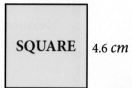
SQUARE
4.6 *cm*

7. Use the domino at the right.
  a. Find the perimeter to the nearest centimeter.
  b. Find the approximate area in centimeters.

8. Use the block at the left.
  a. Find the perimeter to the nearest centimeter.
  b. Find the approximate area in centimeters.

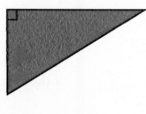

Measure each side of each polygon to the nearest tenth of a centimeter. Find the perimeter of each polygon.

9.

10.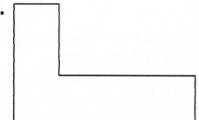

11.

12. The door to Karina's bedroom is 1.07 meters wide by 2.4 meters tall.
  a. What is the perimeter of Karina's door?
  b. What is the area of the door?

13. Omar walked 23.8 meters along one side of a square field.
  a. If he walked the perimeter of this field, how far would he travel?
  b. What is the area of the field?

14. A rectangular card is 14 *cm* long and 10.7 *cm* wide.
   a. What is the perimeter of this card?
   b. What is the area of this card?

Measure all necessary lengths to the nearest tenth of a centimeter. Find the area of each polygon.

15.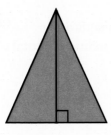

16.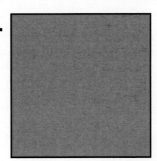

17.

REVIEW

Find the value of each expression. Write in simplest form.

18. $\dfrac{1}{3} \times \dfrac{3}{4}$

19. $\dfrac{7}{10} \div \dfrac{1}{5}$

20. $\dfrac{2}{3} + \dfrac{1}{8}$

21. $\dfrac{14}{15} - \dfrac{3}{5}$

22. $1\frac{2}{5} \div 2\frac{1}{10}$

23. $3\frac{1}{2} \times 1\frac{1}{2}$

24. $2\frac{1}{8} - 1\frac{3}{4}$

25. $4 \div \frac{1}{3}$

26. $2\frac{1}{4} \times 5$

27. A bag containing 15 pounds of grain is divided into $1\frac{2}{3}$ pound portions. How many portions are there?

28. A cat had 6 kittens in one litter. Each kitten weighed approximately $\frac{3}{10}$ of a pound. About how much did all six kittens weigh together?

TIC-TAC-TOE ~ LETTER TO THE EDITOR

The United States of America is one of only a few countries that use customary measurement. The majority of countries in the world use metric measurement. Think about what you have learned about both types of measurement. Which is easier or harder to use? What are the pros and cons of using each type of measurement?

Decide whether you think the United States should continue to use customary measurement or switch to metric measurement. Write a letter to the editor of your local newspaper to explain your choice of measurement. Support your reasons and opinion with examples.

TIC-TAC-TOE ~ COMPOSITE FIGURES

Find the perimeters and areas of composite shapes.

Perimeter – add all sides together

Area – Divide the composite shape into parts or shapes (rectangles, squares or triangles). Find the area of each shape. Then, add all parts together to find the total area.

Find the perimeter and area of each composite shape.

1.

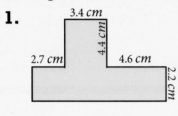

3.4 cm
4.4 cm
2.7 cm   4.6 cm
2.2 cm

Perimeter =
Area =

2.

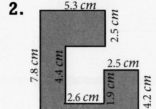

5.3 cm
2.5 cm
7.8 cm
4.4 cm
2.5 cm
2.6 cm
1.9 cm
4.2 cm
7.8 cm

Perimeter =
Area =

3.

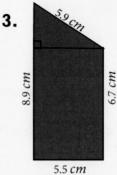

5.9 cm
8.9 cm
6.7 cm
5.5 cm

Perimeter =
Area =

4.

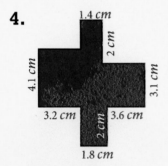

1.4 cm
2 cm
4.1 cm
3.1 cm
3.2 cm   3.6 cm
2 cm
1.8 cm

Perimeter =
Area =

5.

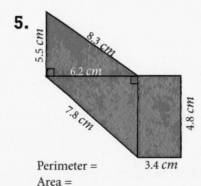

5.5 cm
8.3 cm
6.2 cm
7.8 cm
4.8 cm
3.4 cm

Perimeter =
Area =

6.

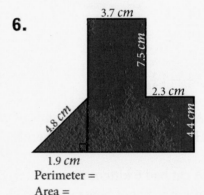

3.7 cm
7.5 cm
2.3 cm
4.8 cm
4.4 cm
1.9 cm

Perimeter =
Area =

Vocabulary

decimal
equivalent decimals

Identify place value of decimals to the thousandths.
Round decimals to the nearest one, tenth, hundredth or thousandth.
Order and compare decimals to find the smallest or largest decimal.
Estimate sums, differences, products or quotients of expressions involving decimals.
Find sums or differences of expressions involving decimals.
Find products of expressions involving decimals.
Find quotients of expressions where decimals are divided by whole numbers.
Find quotients of expressions where decimals are divided by decimals.
Measure and draw line segments using centimeters.
Calculate the perimeter and area of squares, rectangles and triangles using the metric system.

Lesson 21 ~ Place Value with Decimals

Write the decimal that matches each base-ten block model.

1.

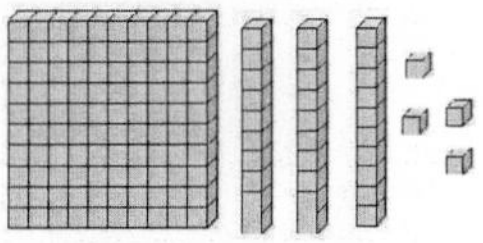

2.

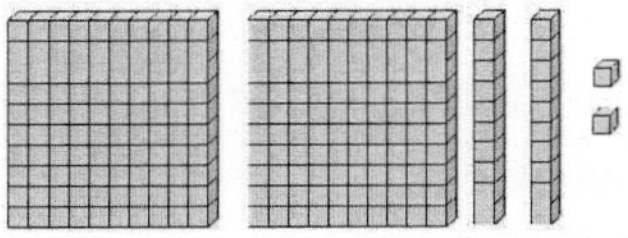

3.

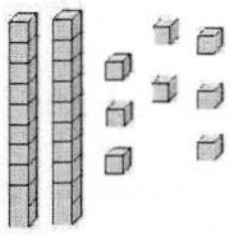

In which place is the digit 5 in each decimal?

4. 15.208

5. 3.521

6. 1.005

Write the decimal for each number in word form.

7. two and seven tenths

8. thirty-four and five hundredths

9. twenty-eight hundredths

Write each decimal in word form.

10. 18.4

11. 9.15

12. 4.004

Lesson 22 ~ Rounding Decimals

Round each decimal to the place value of the digit that is underlined.

13. 52.9<u>8</u>7

14. 3.<u>8</u>43

15. 6.35<u>8</u>6

16. 13.0<u>9</u>8

17. 8.<u>9</u>71

18. <u>6</u>.7

19. 93.0<u>0</u>9

20. 4.<u>0</u>07

21. 5<u>9</u>.99

22. Nadia wants to buy a dress that costs $28.75. Approximately how much money should she bring to the nearest dollar?

23. Elliot buys candy rings for $1.38. How much, to the nearest dime, should he give the cashier?

Lesson 23 ~ Ordering and Comparing Decimals

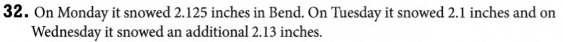

Replace each ⬤ with <, > or = to make a true sentence.

24. 4.3 ⬤ 4.40

25. 70.2 ⬤ 70.23

26. 44.9 ⬤ 44.09

27. 9.53 ⬤ 9.530

28. 8.01 ⬤ 8

29. 11.101 ⬤ 11.0101

Put each set of numbers in order from least to greatest.

30. 9.09, 9.9, 9.009, 9

31. 0.88, 0.8, 0.842, 0.884

32. On Monday it snowed 2.125 inches in Bend. On Tuesday it snowed 2.1 inches and on Wednesday it snowed an additional 2.13 inches.
    a. On what day did it snow the most?
    b. On what day did it snow the least?

Lesson 24 ~ Estimating with Decimals

Estimate each sum, difference or product using rounding to the nearest whole number.

33. 9.6 + 3.4

34. 11.74 − 10.442

35. 6.62 × 4.3

36. 8.98 − 2.76

37. 23.45 + 6.25

38. 10.1 × 10.92

39. Joshua bought three bags of dog food. One bag weighed 4.89 pounds. The other two bags weighed 5.4 pounds and 2.51 pounds. What was the approximate weight of all three bags combined?

Estimate each quotient using compatible numbers.

40. $14.7 \div 7.04$

41. $43.9 \div 5.32$

42. $92.13 \div 9.45$

43. Carlita used 8.14 gallons of gasoline to drive 234.6 miles. Estimate the number of miles she can drive with one gallon of gasoline.

Lesson 25 ~ Adding and Subtracting Decimals

Find each sum or difference.

44. $9.1 + 2.4$

45. $1.981 - 0.682$

46. $31.321 - 28.198$

47. $6.608 + 9.44$

48. $6.71 + 3.32$

49. $4.564 + 8.5$

50. $7.902 - 3.42$

51. $4.86 - 2.9$

52. $14 + 2.57$

53. Brooklyn had a water bottle that contained 16.9 ounces of water. She drank 8.75 ounces of the water. How many ounces were left?

54. Nevaeh measured 2.5 cups of flour and 1.75 cups of sugar into a bowl. How many cups of ingredients did she have altogether in the bowl?

Lesson 26 ~ Multiplying Decimals

Find each product.

55. 7.3×4

56. 3×6.21

57. 5×11.05

58. 3.4×2.6

59. 6.23×4.7

60. 7.14×5.23

61. 0.048×5

62. 8.9×0.039

63. 9.64×0.98

64. Alejandro bought 5.37 pounds of oranges. They cost $0.49 per pound. How much did Alejandro spend on oranges? Round to the nearest penny.

65. Lucia bought games for her video game system. The games cost $19.99 each. How much money did Lucia need for three games?

Lesson 27 ~ Dividing Decimals by Whole Numbers

Find each quotient. Round to the nearest hundredth, if necessary.

66. $9.9 \div 2$

67. $13.53 \div 3$

68. $32.5 \div 5$

69. $2.7 \div 9$

70. $0.88 \div 7$

71. $0.55 \div 10$

72. $19.33 \div 6$ **73.** $54.54 \div 6$ **74.** $38.675 \div 7$

75. Aubrey had 3.5 pounds of ground beef for tacos. She made 25 tacos. How much ground beef did she put into each taco?

Lesson 28 ~ Dividing Decimals by Decimals

Find each quotient. Round to the nearest hundredth, if necessary.

76. $6.7 \div 0.3$ **77.** $14.04 \div 3.2$ **78.** $16.4 \div 2.35$

79. $50.5 \div 0.58$ **80.** $28.92 \div 17.4$ **81.** $33.76 \div 6.56$

82. Kaori spent $99.56 for her cell phone. Yin spent $256.38 to purchase her cell phone. How many times greater was the cost of Yin's cell phone than Kaori's cell phone?

83. Elsa made 3.5 cups of guacamole. A serving of guacamole was 0.125 cup. How many servings did Elsa make?

Lesson 29 ~ Measuring in Centimeters

84. The height of a salt shaker is 14 centimeters and 5 millimeters. Write this measurement as a decimal with centimeter units.

Measure the length of each line to the nearest tenth of a centimeter.

85. ▬▬▬▬▬▬▬▬▬▬▬▬▬▬▬

86. ▬▬▬▬▬▬▬▬▬▬▬▬▬▬▬▬▬▬

87. ▬▬▬

Measure the length of each line to the nearest half centimeter.

88. ▬▬▬▬▬▬▬▬▬▬

89. ▬▬▬

90. ▬▬▬▬▬▬▬▬▬▬▬▬▬▬

91. Use the picture of the lizard.
     a. Estimate the length of the lizard to the nearest tenth of a centimeter.
     b. Measure the length of the lizard to the nearest tenth of a centimeter.
     c. How far off was your estimate, to the nearest tenth of a centimeter?

Draw a line that has each given length.

92. *9 mm*

93. *7.2 cm*

94. *4.6 cm*

Lesson 30 ~ Area and Perimeter with Decimals

• •

Use the given measurements to find each perimeter and area.

95.  *3.2 cm*
4.1 cm

96. SQUARE *7.5 m*

97.  *7.2 mm* *7.2 mm* *6.7 mm* *5.3 mm*

Measure the necessary lengths to the nearest tenth of a centimeter. Find the perimeter and area of each polygon.

98.

99.

100.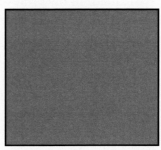

TIC-TAC-TOE ~ BEDROOM AREA

Step 1: Measure the width and length of your bedroom using a metric ruler or measuring tape, to the nearest centimeter. Make a scale drawing of your bedroom where a 1 *cm* line equals 1 meter. Write the measurements as decimals on the outside of the drawing of your bedroom.

Examples: length of 5 meters and 21 centimeters = 5.21 *m*
length of 5 meters and 3 centimeters = 5.03 *m*

Step 2: Measure, to the nearest centimeter, all large items that take up floor space in your room (bed, dresser, chair, desk, etc.) with a metric ruler or measuring tape. Measure at least three items. Draw these items on your scale drawing. Label them with their measurements.

Step 3: Calculate the area of your bedroom.

Step 4: Calculate the floor area each item covers in your bedroom. How much total floor space is left in your room?

Step 5: Rearrange your furniture on paper to maximize your floor space. Are there different ways you could arrange your furniture to give yourself more space? Draw different possible arrangements. You should consult parents or guardians before actually rearranging your bedroom.

CAREER FOCUS

LUIS
ESCROW OFFICER
BEND, OREGON

I am an escrow officer. I deal with legal documents and work with the county to sell and buy homes. In one home purchase transaction I work with realtors, lenders, mortgage brokers, buyers and sellers. My company is a neutral third party that collects information and funds. We keep them until it is time to complete the transaction. Escrow officers are important members of any real estate transaction.

I use basic math in my profession for many things. I add and subtract money that comes in or goes out. I also use ratios to prorate items in transactions. Prorating means to find a part of the whole amount. I prorate taxes and, sometimes, rent for my clients. An example of this is calculating how much tax the buyer and the seller would each need to pay when a house is purchased part way through the year. The amount each one owes is determined with proportions. Math is important in my job to make sure that people are not paying too little or too much.

You must have a high school diploma or equivalent to become an escrow officer. People usually work in an escrow office for 3 or 4 years to gain valuable experience before they become officers.

An escrow officer's salary ranges from $38,000 to $58,000 per year. The salary depends on how experienced they are and how many clients they have.

One thing I like about my profession is the variety of transactions. No sale or refinance is the same. This keeps me busy each day and makes my job interesting. One day I might have a smooth transaction without any problems. Another day I may have a transaction with a lot of obstacles. When there are problems I am like a detective. I try to find out exactly what the problems are and find solutions for them. Another thing that I like about my job is helping people achieve the American Dream of owning a home. This is very rewarding to me.

ACKNOWLEDGEMENTS

All Photos and Clipart ©2008 Jupiterimages Corporation
with the exception of cover photos and the following photos:

Oregon Focus on Fractions and Decimals Page 16
©iStockphoto.com/Lisa F. Young

Oregon Focus on Fractions and Decimals Page 57
©iStockphoto.com/ericsphotography

Oregon Focus on Fractions and Decimals Page 136
©iStockphoto.com/Andres Balacazar

Oregon Focus on Lines and Angles Page 21
©iStockphoto.com/Juan Monino

Oregon Focus on Data Analysis Page 12
©iStockphoto.com/Amanda Rohole

Oregon Focus on Data Analysis Page 79
©iStockphoto.com/Lisa F. Young

Oregon Focus on Proportionality Page 155
©iStockphoto.com/Amanda Rohole

Layout and Design by JS Data Designs

Design Support by Heather Day

Cover Design by Schuyler St. Lawrence

Glossary Translation by Keyla Santiago

Special thanks to the participants in the Career Focus pages for their willingness to share about their jobs.

Very special thanks to our spouses and families who put up with us during one crazy year of curriculum writing and editing. We couldn't have done it without your support!

Absolute Value	The distance a number is from 0 on a number line.	Valor Absoluto	La distancia de un número desde el 0 en una recta numérica.
Acute Angle	An angle that measures more than 0° but less than 90°.	Ángulos Agudos	Un ángulo que mide mas 0° pero menos de 90°.
Adjacent Angles	Two angles that share a ray.	Ángulos Adyacentes	Dos ángulos que comparten un rayo.
Algebraic Expression	An expression that contains numbers, operations and variables.	Expresiones Algebraicas	Una expresión que contiene números, operaciones y variables.
Alternate Exterior Angles	Two angles that are on the outside of two lines and are on opposites sides of a transversal.	Ángulos Exteriores Alternos	Dos ángulos que están afuera de dos rectas y están a lados opuestos de una transversal.
Alternate Interior Angles	Two angles that are on the inside of two lines and are on opposites sides of a transversal.	Ángulos Interiores Alternos	Dos ángulos que están adentro de dos rectas y están a lados opuestos de una transversal.
Angle	A figure formed by two rays with a common endpoint.	Ángulo	Una figura formada por dos rayos con un punto final en común.
Area	The number of square units needed to cover a surface.	Área	El número de unidades cuadradas necesitadas para cubrir una superficie.

Ascending Order	Numbers arranged from least to greatest.	Progresión Ascendente	Los números ordenados de menor a mayor.
Associative Property	A property that states that numbers in addition or multiplication expressions can be grouped without affecting the value of the expression.	Propiedad Asociativa	Una propiedad que establece que los números en expresiones de suma o de multiplicación pueden ser agrupados sin afectar el valor de la expresión.
Axes	A horizontal and vertical number line on a coordinate plane.	Ejes	Una recta numérica horizontal y vertical en un plano de coordenadas.

B

Bar Graph	A graph that uses bars to compare the quantities in a categorical data set.	Gráfico de Barras	Una gráfica que utiliza barras para comparar las cantidades en un conjunto de datos categórico.
Base of a Power	The repeated factor in a power.	Base de un Potencia	El factor repetido en una potencia.
Base of a Solid	See Prism, Cylinder, Pyramid and Cone.	Base de un Sólido	Ver Prisma, Cilindro, Pirámide y Cono.
Base of a Triangle	Any side of a triangle.	Base de un Triángulo.	Cualquier lado de un Triángulo.
Bias	A problem when gathering data that affects the results of the data.	Sesgo	Un problema que ocurre cuando se recogen datos que afectan los resultados de los datos.

| Box-and-Whisker Plot | A diagram used to display the five-number summary of a data set. | Diagrama de Líneas y Bloques | Un diagrama utilizado para mostrar el resumen de cinco números de un conjunto de datos. |

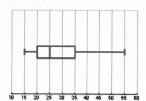
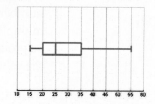

C

| Categorical Data | Data collected in the form of words. | Datos Categóricos | Datos recopilados en la forma de palabras. |

| Center of a circle | The point inside a circle that is the same distance from all points on the circle. | Centro de un Círculo | Un ángulo dentro de un círculo que está a la misma distancia de todos los puntos en el círculo. |

| Central Angle | An angle in a circle with its vertex at the center of the circle. | Ángulo Central | Un ángulo en un círculo con su vértice en el centro del círculo. |

| Chord | A line segment with endpoints on the circle. | Cuerda | Un segmento de la recta con puntos finales en el círculo. |

| Circle | The set of all points that are the same distance from a center point. | Círculo | El conjunto de todos los puntos que están a la misma distancia de un punto central. |

| Circumference | The distance around a circle. | Circunferencia | La distancia alrededor de un círculo. |

| Coefficient | The number multiplied by a variable in a term. | Coeficiente | El número multiplicado por una variable en un término. |

Commutative Property	A property that states numbers can be added or multiplied in any order.	Propiedad Conmutativa	Una propiedad que establece que los números pueden ser sumados o multiplicados en cualquier orden.
Compatible Numbers	Numbers that are easy to mentally compute; used when estimating products and quotients	Números Compatibles	Números que son fáciles de calcular mentalmente; utilizado cuando se estiman productos y cocientes.
Complementary Angles	Two angles whose sum is 90°.	Ángulos Complementarios	Dos ángulos cuya suma es de 90°.
Complements	Two probabilities whose sum is 1. Together they make up all the possible outcomes without repeating any outcomes.	Complementos	Dos probabilidades cuya suma es de 1. Juntos crean todos los posibles resultados sin repetir alguno.
Composite Figure	A geometric figure made of two or more geometric shapes.	Figura Compuesta	Una figura geométrica formada por dos o más formas geométricas.
Composite Number	A whole number larger than 1 that has more than two factors.	Número Compuesto	Un número entero mayor que el 1 con más de dos factores.
Composite Solid	A solid made of two or more three-dimensional geometric figures.	Sólido Compuesto	Un sólido formado por dos o más figuras geométricas tridimensionales.
Cone	A solid formed by one circular base and a vertex.	Cono	Un sólido formado por una base circular y una vértice.

Congruent	Equal in measure.	Congruente	Igual en medida.
Congruent Figures	Two shapes that have the exact same shape and the exact same size.	Figuras Congruentes	Dos figuras que tienen exactamente la misma forma y el mismo tamaño.

Constant	A term that has no variable.	Constante	Un término que no tiene variable.

Continuous	When a graph can be drawn from beginning to end without any breaks.	Continuo	Cuando una gráfica puede ser dibujada desde principio a fin sin ninguna interrupción.
Conversion	The process of renaming a measurement using different units.	Conversión	El proceso de renombrar una medida utilizando diferentes unidades.
Coordinate Plane	A plane created by two number lines intersecting at a 90° angle.	Plano de Coordenadas	Un plano creado por dos rectas numéricas que se intersecan a un ángulo de 90°.

Correlation	The relationship between two variables in a scatter plot.	Correlación	La relación entre dos variables en un gráfico de dispersión.
Corresponding Angles	Two non-adjacent angles that are on the same side of a transversal with one angle inside the two lines and the other on the outside of the two lines.	Ángulos Correspondientes	Dos ángulos no adyacentes que están en el mismo lado de una transversal con un ángulo adentro de las dos rectas y el otro afuera de las dos rectas.

Corresponding Parts	The angles and sides in similar or congruent figures that match.	Partes Correspondientes	Los ángulos y lados en figuras similares o congruentes que concuerdan.
Cubed	A number to the third power.	Elevado al Cubo	Un número elevado a la tercera potencia.
Cylinder	A solid formed by two congruent and parallel circular bases.	Cilindro	Un sólido formado por dos bases circulares congruentes y paralelas.

D

Decimal	A number with a digit in the tenths place, hundredths place, etc.	Decimal	Un número con un dígito en las décimas, las centenas, etc.
Degrees	A unit used to measure angles.	Grados	Una unidad utilizada para medir ángulos.
Descending Order	Numbers arranged from greatest to least.	Progresión Descendente	Los números ordenados de mayor a menor.
Diameter	The distance across a circle through the center.	Diámetro	La distancia a través de un círculo por el centro.

Direct Variation	A linear function that passes through the origin and has equation $y=mx$.	Variación Directa	Una función lineal que pasa a través del origen y tiene la ecuación $y=mx$.
Discount	The decrease in the price of an item.	Descuento	La disminución de precio en un artículo.
Discrete	When a graph can be represented by a unique set of points rather than a continuous line.	Discreto	Cuando una gráfica puede ser representada por un conjunto de puntos único en vez de una recta continua.
Distance Formula	A formula used to find the distance between two points on the coordinate plane.	Fórmula de Distancia	Una fórmula utilizada para encontrar la distancia entre dos puntos en un plano de coordenadas.

$$d = \sqrt{(x_2 - x_1)^2 + (y_2 - y_1)^2}$$

$$d = \sqrt{(x_2 - x_1)^2 + (y_2 - y_1)^2}$$

Distributive Property	A property that can be used to rewrite an expression without parentheses: $a(b + c) = a \times b + a \times c$	Propiedad Distributiva	Una propiedad que puede ser utilizada para reescribir una expresión sin paréntesis: $a(b + c) = a \times b + a \times c$
Dividend	The number being divided Example: $100 \div 4 = 25$	Dividendo	El número que es dividido. Ejemplo: $100 \div 4 = 25$
Divisor	The number used to divide Example: $100 \div 4 = 25$	Divisor	El número utilizado para dividir. Ejemplo: $100 \div 4 = 25$

Double Stem-and-Leaf Plot	A stem-and-leaf plot where one set of data is placed on the right side of the stem and another is placed on the left of the stem.	Doble Gráfica de Tallo y Hoja	Una gráfica de tallo y hoja donde un conjunto de datos es colocado al lado derecho del tallo y el otro es colocado a la izquierda del tallo.
	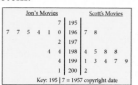		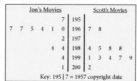

E

Edge	The segment where two faces of a solid meet. 	Arista (Borde)	El segmento donde dos caras de un sólido se encuentran. 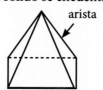
Elimination Method	A method for solving a system of linear equations.	Método de Eliminación	Un método para resolver un sistema de ecuaciones lineales.
Equally Likely	Two or more possible outcomes of a given situation that have the same probability.	Igualmente Probables	Dos o más posibles resultados de una situación dada que tienen la misma probabilidad.
Equation	A mathematical sentence that contains an equals sign between 2 expressions.	Ecuación	Una oración matemática que contiene un símbolo de igualdad entre dos expresiones.
Equiangular	A polygon in which all angles are congruent.	Equiángulo	Un polígono en el cual todos los ángulos son congruentes.
Equilateral	A polygon in which all sides are congruent. 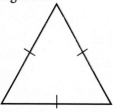	Equilátero	Un polígono en el cual todos los lados son congruentes. 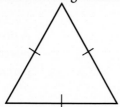
Equivalent Decimals	Two or more decimals that represent the same number.	Decimales Equivalentes	Dos o más decimales que representan el mismo número.
Equivalent Expressions	Two or more expressions that represent the same algebraic expression.	Expresiones Equivalentes	Dos o más expresiones que representan la misma expresión algebraica.

Equivalent Fractions	Two or more fractions that represent the same number.	Fracciones Equivalentes	Dos o más fracciones que representan el mismo número.
Evaluate	To find the value of an expression.	Evaluar	Encontrar el valor de una expresión.
Even Distribution	A set of data values that is evenly spread across the range of the data.	Distribución Igualada	Un conjunto de valores de datos que es esparcido de modo uniforme a través de la extensión de los datos.
Event	A desired outcome or group of outcomes.	Suceso	Un resultado o grupo de resultados deseados.
Experimental Probability	The ratio of the number of times an event occurs to the total number of trials.	Probabilidad Experimental	La razón de la cantidad de veces que un suceso ocurre a la cantidad total de intentos.
Exponent	The number of times a factor is repeated in a power.	Exponente	La cantidad de veces que un factor es repetido en una potencia.

F

Face	A polygon that is a side or base of a solid.	Cara	Un polígono que es una base de lado de un sólido.

face

cara

Factors	Whole numbers that can be multiplied together to find a product.	Factores	Números enteros que pueden ser multiplicados entre si para encontrar un producto.
First Quartile (Q1)	The median of the lower half of a data set.	Primer Cuartil (Q1)	Mediana de la parte inferior de un conjunto de datos.
Five-Number Summary	Describes the spread of a data set using the minimum, 1st quartile, median, 3rd quartile,and maximum.	Resumen de Cinco Números	Describe la extensión de un conjunto de datos utilizando el mínimo, el primer cuartil, la mediana el tercer cuartil y el máximo.
Formula	An algebraic equation that shows the relationship amoung specific quantities.	Fórmula	Una ecuación algebraica que enseña la relación entre cantidades específicas.
Fraction	A number that represents a part of a whole number, written as numerator/ denominator.	Fracción	Un número que representa una parte de un número entero, escrito como numerador/denominador.

| Frequency | The number a times an item occurs in a data set. | Frecuencia | La cantidad de veces que un artículo ocurre en un conjunto de datos. |

| Frequency Table | A table which shows how many times a value occurs in a given interval. | Tabla de Frecuencia | Una tabla que enseña cuantas veces un valor ocurre en un intervalo dado. |

Weight of Newborn (in Pounds)	Tally
4 – 5.5	I
5.5 – 7	III
7 – 8.5	NHH
8.5 – 10	II
10 – 11.5	I

| Function | A pairing of input and output values according to a specific rule. | Función | El emparejamiento de valores de entrada y salida de acuerdo a una regla específica. |

G

| Geometric Probability | Ratios of lengths or areas used to find the likelihood of an event. | Probabilidad Geométrica | Razones de longitudes o áreas utilizadas para encontrar la probabilidad de un suceso. |

| Geometric Sequence | A list of numbers created by multiplying the previous term in the sequence by a common ratio. | Secuencia Geométrica | Una lista de números creada al multiplicar el término anterior en la secuencia por una razón común. |

| Greatest Common Factor (GCF) | The greatest factor that is common to two or more numbers. | Máximo Común Divisor (MCD) | El máximo divisor que le es común a dos o más números. |

| Grouping Symbols | Symbols such as parentheses or fraction bars that group parts of an expressions. | Símbolos de Agrupación | Símbolos como el paréntesis o barras de fracción que agrupan las partes de una expresión. |

H

| Height of a Triangle | A perpendicular line drawn from the side whose length is the base to the opposite vertex. | Altura de un Triángulo | Una recta perpendicular dibujada desde el lado cuya longitud es la base al vértice opuesto. |

Histogram	A bar graph that displays the frequency of numerical data in equal-sized intervals.	Histograma	Un gráfico de barras que muestra la frecuencia de datos numéricos en intervalos de tamaños iguales.

Hypotenuse	The side opposite the right angle in a right triangle.	Hipotenusa	El lado opuesto el ángulo recto en un triángulo rectángulo.

I-J-K

Improper Fraction	A fraction whose numerator is greater than or equal to its denominator.	Fracción Impropia	Una fracción cuyo numerador es mayor o igual a su denominador.
Input-Output Table	A table used to describe a function by listing input values with their output values.	Tabla de Entrada y Salida	Una tabla utilizada para describir una función al enumerar valores de entrada con sus valores de salidas.

Input, x	Output, y

Input, x	Output, y

Integers	The set of all whole numbers, their opposites, and 0.	Enteros	El conjunto de todos los números enteros, sus opuestos y 0.
Interquartile Range (IQR)	The difference between the 3rd quartile and the 1st quartile in a set of data.	Rango Intercuartil (IQR)	La diferencia entre el tercer cuartil y el primer cuartil en un conjunto de datos.
Inverse Operations	Operations that undo each other.	Operaciones Inversas	Operaciones que se cancelan la una a la otra.
IQR Method	A method for determining outliers.	Método IQR	Un método para determinar los datos aberrantes.
Irrational Numbers	A number that cannot be expressed as a fraction of two integers.	Números Irracionales	Un número que no puede ser expresado como una fracción de dos enteros.

Isosceles Trapezoid	A trapezoid that has congruent legs. 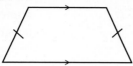	Trapezoide Isósceles	Un trapezoide con catetos congruentes. 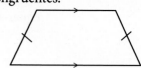
Isosceles Triangle	A triangle that has two or more congruent sides. 	Triángulo Isósceles	Un triángulo que tiene dos o más lados congruentes.

L

Lateral Face	A side of a solid that is not a base.	Cara Lateral	Un lado de un sólido que no sea una base.
Least Common Denominator (LCD)	The least common multiple of two or more denominators.	Mínimo Común Denominador (MCD)	El mínimo común múltiplo de dos o más denominadores.
Least Common Multiple (LCM)	The smallest nonzero multiple that is common to two or more numbers.	Mínimo Común Múltiplo (MCM)	El múltiplo más pequeño que no sea cero que le es común a dos o más números.
Leg	The two sides of a right triangle that form a right angle. 	Cateto	Los dos lados de un triángulo rectángulo que forman un ángulo recto. 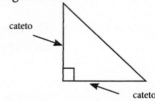
Like Terms	Terms that have the same variable(s).	Términos Semejantes	Términos que tienen el mismo variable(s).
Line of Best Fit	A line which best represents the pattern of a two-variable data set. 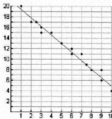	Recta de Mejor Ajuste	Una recta que mejor representa el patrón de un conjunto de datos de dos variables. 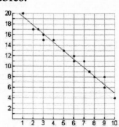

Linear Equation	An equation whose graph is a line.	Ecuación Lineal	Una ecuación cuya gráfica es una recta.
Linear Function	A function whose graph is a line.	Función Lineal	Una función cuya gráfica es una recta.
Linear Pair	Two adjacent angles whose non-common sides are opposite rays.	Par Lineal	Dos ángulos adyacentes cuyos lados no comunes son rayos opuestos.

M

Markup	The increase in the price of an item.	Margen de Beneficio	El aumento de precio en un artículo.
Mean	The sum of all values in a data set divided by the number of values.	Media	La suma de todos los valores en un conjunto de datos dividido entre la cantidad de valores.
Measures of Center	Numbers that are used to represent a data set with a single value; the mean, median, and mode are the measures of center.	Medidas de Centro	Números que son utilizados para representar un conjunto de datos con un solo valor; la media, la mediana, y la moda son las medidas de centro.
Median	The middle number or the average of the two middle numbers in an ordered data set.	Mediana	El número medio o el promedio de los dos números medios en un conjunto de datos ordenados.
Mixed Number	The sum of a whole number and a fraction less than 1.	Números Mixtos	La suma de un número entero y una fracción menor que 1.
Mode	The number(s) or item(s) that occur most often in a data set.	Moda	El número(s) o artículo(s) que ocurre con más frecuencia en un conjunto de datos.
Motion Rate	A rate that compares distance to time	Índice de Movimiento	Un índice que compara distancia por tiempo.
Multiple	The product of a number and nonzero whole number.	Múltiplo	El producto de un número y un número entero que no sea cero.

N

Negative Number	A numbers less than 0.	Número Negativo	Un número menor que 0.

Net	A two-dimensional pattern that folds to form a solid.	Red	Un patrón bidimensional que se dobla para formar un sólido.

Non-Linear Function	A function whose graph does not form a line.	Ecuación No Lineal	Una ecuación cuya gráfica no forma una recta.
Normal Distribution	A set of data values where the majority of the values are located in the middle of the data set and can be displayed by a bell-shaped curve.	Distribución Normal	Un conjunto de valores de datos donde la mayoría de los valores están localizados en el medio del conjunto de datos y pueden ser mostrados por una curva de forma de campana.
Numerical Data	Data collected in the form of numbers.	Datos Numéricos	Datos recopilados en la forma de números.
Numerical Expressions	An expression consisting of numbers and operations that represents a specific value.	Expresiones Numéricas	Una expresión que consta de números y operaciones que representa un valor específico.

O

Obtuse Angle	An angle that measures more than 90° but less than 180°.	Ángulo Obtuso	Un ángulo que mide más de 90° pero menos de 180°.

Opposites	Numbers the same distance from 0 on a number line but are on opposite sides of 0.	Opuestos	Números a la misma distancia del 0 en un recta numérica pero en lados opuestos del 0.
Order of Operations	The rules to follow when evaluating an expression with more than one operation.	Orden de las Operaciones	Las reglas a seguir cuando se evalúa una expresión con más de una operación.
Ordered Pair	A pair of numbers used to locate a point on a coordinate plane (x, y).	Pares Ordenados	Un par de números utilizados para localizar un punto en un plano de coordenadas (x,y).

Origin	The point where the *x*- and *y*-axis intersect on a coordinate plane (0, 0).	Origen	El punto donde el eje de la *x*- y el de la *y*- se cruzan en un plano de coordenadas (0,0).

origin

origen

Outcome	One possible result from an experiment or probability event.	Resultado	Un resultado posible de un experimento o un suceso de probabilidad.
Outlier	An extreme value that varies greatly from the other values in a data set.	Dato Aberrante	Un valor extremo que varía mucho de los otros valores en un conjunto de datos.

P

Parallel	Lines in the same plane that never intersect.	Paralela	Rectas en el mismo plano que nunca se intersecan.
Parallel Box-and-Whisker Plot	One box-and-whisker plot placed above another used to compare data sets.	Diagrama Paralelo de Líneas y Bloques	Un diagrama de líneas y bloques ubicado sobre otro para comparar conjuntos de datos.

Number of Rebounds per Game

Number of Rebounds per Game

Parallelogram	A quadrilateral with both pairs of opposite sides parallel.	Paralelogramo	Un cuadrilateral con ambos pares de lados opuestos paralelos.

Parent Graph	The most basic graph of a function.	Gráfico Matriz	La gráfica más básica de una función.
Percent	A ratio that compares a number to 100.	Por ciento	Una razón que compara un número con 100.
Percent of Change	The percent a quantity increases or decreases compared to the original amount.	Por ciento de Cambio	El por ciento que una cantidad aumenta o disminuye comparado a la cantidad original.

Percent of Decrease	The percent of change when the new amount is less than the original amount.	Por ciento de Disminución	El por ciento de cambio cuando la nueva cantidad es menos que la cantidad original.
Percent of Increase	The percent of change when the new amount is more than the original amount.	Por ciento de Incremento	El por ciento de cambio cuando la nueva cantidad es más que la cantidad original.
Perfect Square	A number whose square root is an integer.	Cuadrado Perfecto	Un número cuya raíz cuadrada es un entero.
Perimeter	The distance around a figure.	Perímetro	La distancia alrededor de una figura.
Perpendicular	Two lines or segments that form a right angle.	Perpendicular	Dos rectas o segmentos que forman un ángulo recto.

Pi (π)	The ratio of the circumference of a circle to its diameter.	Pi (π)	La razón de la circunferencia de un círculo a su diámetro.
Pictograph	A graph that uses pictures to compare the amounts represented in a categorical data set.	Gráfica Pictórica	Una gráfica que utiliza dibujos para comparar las cantidades representadas en un conjunto de datos categóricos.

Pie Chart	A circle graph that shows information as sectors of a circle.	Gráfico Circular	Enseña la información como sectores de un círculo.

Polygon	A closed figure formed by three or more line segments.	Polígono	Una figura cerrada formada por tres o más segmentos de rectas.

| Positive Number | A number greater than 0. | Número Positivo | Un número mayor que 0. |

Power — An expression using an exponent that represents the product of a repeated factor.

Potencia — Una expresión que utiliza un exponente que representa el producto de un factor repetido.

Prime Factorization — When any composite number is written as the product of all its prime factors

Factorización Prima — Cuando cualquier número compuesto es escrito como el producto de todos los factores primos.

Prime Number — A whole number larger than 1 that has only two possible factors, 1 and itself.

Número Primo — Un número entero mayor que 1 que tiene solo dos factores posibles, 1 y el mismo.

Prism — A solid formed by polygons with two congruent, parallel bases.

Prisma — Un sólido formado por polígonos con dos bases congruentes y paralelas.

Probability — The measure of how likely it is an event will occur.

Probabilidad — La medida de cuán probable un suceso puede ocurrir.

Proper Fraction — A fraction with a numerator that is less than the denominator.

Fracción Propia — Una fracción con un numerador que es menos que el denominador.

Proportion — An equation stating two ratios are equivalent.

Proporción — Una ecuación que establece que dos razones son equivalentes.

Protractor — A tool used to measure angles.

Transportador — Una herramienta para medir ángulos.

Pyramid — A solid with a polygonal base and triangular sides that meet at a vertex.

Pirámide — Un sólido con una base poligonal y lados triangulares que se encuentran en un vértice.

| Pythagorean Triple | A set of three positive integers (a, b, c) such that $a^2 + b^2 = c^2$. | Triple de Pitágoras | Un conjunto de tres enteros positivos (a, b, c) tal que $a^2 + b^2 = c^2$ |

Q

| Q-Points | Points that are created by the intersection of the quartiles for the x- and y-values of a two-variable data set. | Puntos Q | Puntos que son creados por la intersección de los cuartiles para los valores de la x- y la y- de un conjunto de datos de dos variables. |
| Quadrants | Four regions formed by the x and x axes on a coordinate plane. | Cuadrantes | Cuatro regiones formadas por el eje-x y el eje-y en un plano de coordenadas. |

| Quadrilateral | A polygon with four sides | Cuadrilateral | Un polígono con cuatro lados. |
| Quotient | The answer to a division problem. | Cociente | La solución a un problema de división. |

R

| Radius | The distance from the center of a circle to any point on the circle. | Radio | La distancia desde el centro de un círculo a cualquier punto en el círculo. |

Random Sample	A sample that is representative of the population being studied, with each person or object having an equal chance of being included.	Muestra Aleatoria	Una muestra que representa a la población que es estudiada; cada persona o objeto tiene la misma oportunidad de ser incluido.
Range	The difference between the maximum and minimum values in a data set.	Extensión	La diferencia entre los valores máximo y mínimo en un conjunto de datos.
Rate	A ratio of two numbers that have different units.	Índice	Una proporción de dos números con diferentes unidades.

| Rate Conversion | A process of changing at least one unit of measurement in a rate to a different unit of measurement. | Conversión de Índice | Un proceso de cambiar por lo menos una unidad de medición en un índice a una diferente unidad de medición. |

| Rate of Change | The change in y-values over the change in x-values on a linear graph. | Índice de Cambio | El cambio en los valores de y sobre el cambio en los valores de x en una gráfica lineal. |

| Ratio | A comparison of two numbers using division. $a:b$ $\frac{a}{b}$ a to b | Razón | Una comparación de dos números utilizando división. $a:b$ $\frac{a}{b}$ a to b |

| Rational Number | A number that can be expressed as a fraction of two integers. | Número Racional | Un número que puede ser expresado como una fracción de dos enteros. |

| Ray | A part of a line that has one endpoint and extends forever in one direction. | Rayo | Una parte de una recta que tiene un punto final y se extiende eternamente en una dirección. |

| Real Numbers | The set of numbers that includes all rational and irrational numbers. | Números Racionales | El conjunto de números que incluye todos los números racionales e irracionales. |

| Reciprocals | Two numbers whose product is 1. | Recíprocos | Dos números cuyo producto es 1. |

| Recursive Routine | A routine described by stating the start value and the operation performed to get the following terms. | Rutina Recursiva | Una rutina descrita al exponer el valor del comienzo y la operación realizada para conseguir los términos siguientes. |

| Recursive Sequence | An ordered list of numbers created by a first term and a repeated operation. | Secuencia Recursiva | Una lista de números ordenados creada por un primer término y una operación repetida. |

| Repeating Decimal | A decimal that has one or more digits that repeat forever. | Decimal Repetitivo | Un decimal que tiene uno o más dígitos que se repiten eternamente. |

| Right Angle | An angle that measures 90°. | Ángulo Recto | Un ángulo que mide 90°. |

Sales Tax	An amount added to the cost of an item. The amount added is a percent of the original amount as determined by a state, county, or city.	Impuesto sobre las Ventas	Una cantidad añadida al costo de un artículo. La cantidad añadida es un por ciento de la cantidad original determinado por el estado, condado o ciudad.
Same-Side Interior Angles	Two angles that are on the inside of two lines and are on the same side of a transversal.	Ángulos Interiores del Mismo Lado	Dos ángulos que están en el interior de dos rectas y están en el mismo lado de una transversal.
Sample	A part of the population that is used to make conclusions about the entire population.	Muestra	Una parte de la población que es utilizada para formular conclusiones de la población entera.
Sample Space	The set of all possible outcomes for an event.	Muestra de Espacio	El conjunto de todos los posibles resultados para un suceso.
Scale	The ratio of a length on a map or model to the actual object.	Escala	La razón de una longitud en un mapa o modelo al objeto verdadero.
Scale Factor	The ratio of corresponding sides in two similar figures.	Factor de Escala	La razón de los lados correspondientes en dos figuras similares.
Scalene Triangle	A triangle that has no congruent sides.	Triángulo Escaleno	Un triángulo sin lados congruentes.
Scatter Plot	A set of ordered pairs graphed on a coordinate plane.	Diagrama de Dispersión	Un conjunto de pares ordenados graficados en un plano de coordenadas.

| Scientific Notation | A way of writing extremely large or small numbers as the product of a number between 1 and 10 and a power of 10. | Notación Científica | Una manera de escribir números extremadamente grandes o pequeños como el producto de un número entre 1 y 10 y una potencia de 10. |

| Sector | A portion of a circle enclosed by two radii. | Sector | Una porción de un circulo encerado por dos radios. |

| Sequence | An ordered list of numbers. | Sucesión | Una lista de números ordenados. |

| Similar Figures | Two figures that have the exact same shape, but not necessarily the exact same size. | Figuras Similares | Dos figuras que tienen exactamente la misma forma, pero no necesariamente el mismo tamaño exacto. |

| Similar Solids | Solids that have the same shape and all corresponding dimensions are proportional. | Sólidos Similares | Sólidos con la misma forma y todas sus dimensiones correspondientes son proporcionales. |

| Simplest Form | A fraction whose numerator and denominator's only common factor is 1. | Expresión Mínima | Una fracción cuyo único factor común del numerador y del denominador es 1. |

| Simplify an Expression | To rewrite an expression without parentheses and combine all like terms. | Simplificar una Expresión | Reescribir una expresión sin paréntesis y combinar todos los términos iguales. |

| Single-Variable Data | A data set with only one type of data. | Datos de una Variable | Un conjunto de datos con tan solo un tipo de datos. |

| Sketch | To make a figure free hand without the use of measurement tools. | Esbozo | Hacer una figura a mano libre sin utilizar herramientas de medidas. |

English		Spanish	
Skewed Left	A plot or graph with a longer tail on the left-hand side.	Torcido a la Izquierda	Un gráfico con una cola al lado izquierdo.
Skewed Right	A plot or graph with a longer tail on the right-hand side.	Torcido a la Derecha	Un gráfico con una cola al lado derecho.
Slant Height	The height of a lateral face of a pyramid or cone.	Altura Sesgada	La altura de un cara lateral de una pirámide o cono.

Slope	The ratio of the vertical change to the horizontal change in a linear graph.	Pendiente	La razón del cambio vertical al cambio horizontal en una gráfica lineal.
Slope Triangle	A right triangle formed where one leg represents the vertical rise and the other leg is the horizontal run in a linear graph.	Triángulo de Pendiente	Un triángulo rectángulo formado donde una cateto representa el ascenso y la otra es una carrera horizontal en una gráfica lineal.

Slope-Intercept Form	A linear equation written in the form $y = mx + b$.	Forma de las Intersecciones con la Pendiente	Una ecuación lineal escrita en la forma $y = mx + b$.
Solid	A three-dimensional figure that encloses a part of space.	Sólido	Una figura tridimensional que encierra una parte del espacio.
Solution	Any value or values that makes an equation true.	Solución	Cualquier valor o valores que hacen una ecuación verdadera.
Solution of a System of Linear Equations	The ordered pair that satisfies both linear equations in the system.	Solución de un Sistema de Ecuaciones Lineales	El par ordenado que satisface ambas ecuaciones lineales en el sistema.

Sphere	A solid formed by a set of points in space that are the same distance from a center point.	Esfera	Un sólido formado por un conjunto de puntos en el espacio que están a la misma distancia de un punto central.

Square Root	One of the two equal factors of a number. $$25 = 5 \cdot 5 \qquad \sqrt{25} = 5$$	Raíz Cuadrada	Uno de los factores iguales de un número. $$25 = 5 \cdot 5 \qquad \sqrt{25} = 5$$
Squared	A number to the second power.	al Cuadrado	Un número a la segunda potencia.
Start Value	The output value that is paired with an input value of 0 in an input-output table.	Valor de Comienzo	El valor de salida que es aparejado con un valor de entrada de 0 en una tabla de entradas y salidas.
Statistics	The process of collecting, displaying, and analyzing a set of data.	Estadísticas	El proceso de recopilar, exponer y analizar un conjunto de datos.
Stem-and-Leaf Plot	A plot which uses the digits of the data values to show the shape and distribution of the data set.	Gráfica de Tallo y Hoja	Un diagrama que utiliza los dígitos de los valores de datos para mostrar la forma y la distribución del conjunto de datos.

```
 5 | 6
 6 |
 7 | 5  2  9  9
 8 | 0  6  0  8  9
 9 | 3  4  2  8
10 | 0  0
Key: 7 | 5 = 75
```

```
 5 | 6
 6 |
 7 | 5  2  9  9
 8 | 0  6  0  8  9
 9 | 3  4  2  8
10 | 0  0
Key: 7 | 5 = 75
```

Straight Angle	An angle that measures 180°.	Ángulo Llano	Un ángulo que mide 180°.
Substitution Method	A method for solving a system of linear equations.	Método de Substitución	Un método para resolver un sistema de ecuaciones lineales.
Supplementary Angles	Two angles whose sum is 180°	Ángulos Suplementarios	Dos ángulos cuya suma es 180°.
Surface Area	The sum of the areas of all the surfaces on a solid.	Área de la Superficie	La suma de las áreas de todas las superficies en un sólido.
System of Linear Equations	Two or more linear equations.	Sistema de Ecuaciones Lineales	Dos o más ecuaciones lineales.

T

Term	A number or the product of a number and a variable in an algebraic expression; A number in a sequence.	Término	Un número o el producto de un número y una variable en una expresión algebraica; Un número en una sucesión.
Terminating Decimal	A decimal that stops.	Decimal Finito	Un decimal que para.
Theorem	A relationship in mathematics that has been proven.	Teorema	Una relación en las matemáticas que ha sido probada.
Theoretical Probability	The ratio of favorable outcomes to the number of possible outcomes.	Probabilidad Teórica	La proporción de resultados favorables a la cantidad de resultados posibles.
Third Quartile (Q3)	The median of the upper half of a data set.	Tercer Cuartil (Q3)	Mediana de la parte superior de un conjunto de datos.
Tick Marks	Equally divided spaces marked with a small line between every inch or centimeter on a ruler.	Marcas de Graduación	Espacios divididos igualmente marcados con una línea pequeña entre cada pulgada o centímetro en una regla.
Transversal	A line that intersects two or more lines in the same plane.	Transversal	Una recta que interseca dos o más rectas en el mismo plano.
Trapezoid	A quadrilateral with exactly one pair of parallel sides.	Trapezoide	Un cuadrilatero con exactamente un par de lados paralelos.
Trial	A single act of performing an experiment.	Prueba	Un solo intento de realizar un experimento.
Two-Step Equation	An equation that has two different operations.	Ecuación de Dos Pasos	Una ecuación que tiene dos operaciones diferentes.
Two-Variable Data	A data set where two groups of numbers are looked at simultaneously.	Datos de dos Variables	Un conjunto de datos dónde dos grupos de números se observan simultáneamente.

U-V-W-X-Y-Z

| Unit Rate | A rate with a denominator of 1. | Índice de Unidad | Un índice con un denominador de 1. |

| Variable | A symbol that represents one or more numbers | Variable | Un símbolo que representa uno o más números. |

Vertex of a Solid — The point where three or more edges meet.

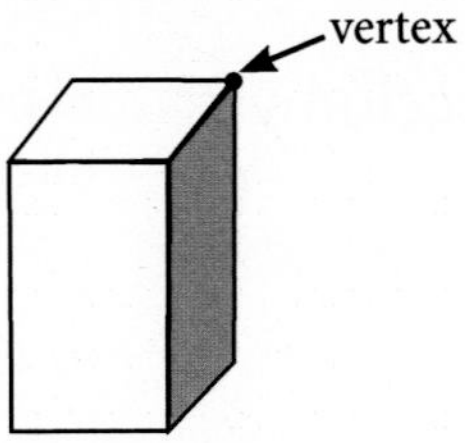

vertex

Vértice de un Sólido — El punto donde tres o más bordes se encuentran.

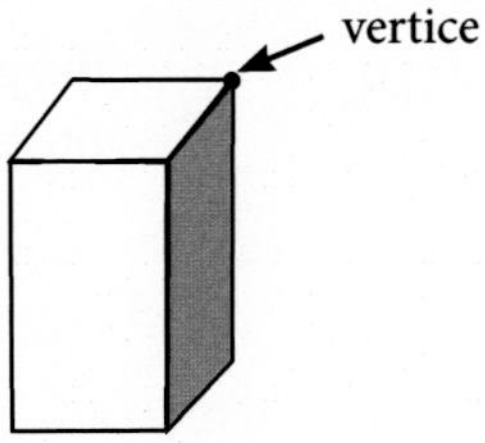

vertice

Vertex of a Triangle — A point where two sides of a triangle meet.

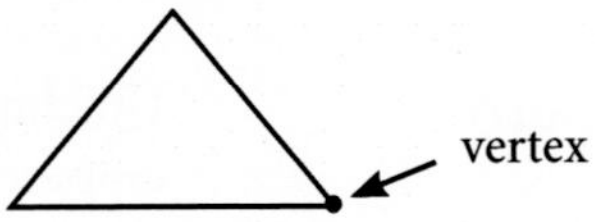

vertex

Vértice de un Triángulo — Un punto donde dos lados de un triángulo se encuentran.

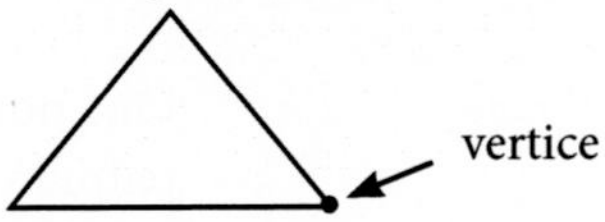

vertice

Vertex of an Angle — The common endpoint of the two rays that form an angle.

vertex

Vértice de un Ángulo — El punto final en común de los dos rayos que forma un ángulo.

vertice

Vertical Angles — Nonadjacent angles with a common vertex formed by two intersecting lines.

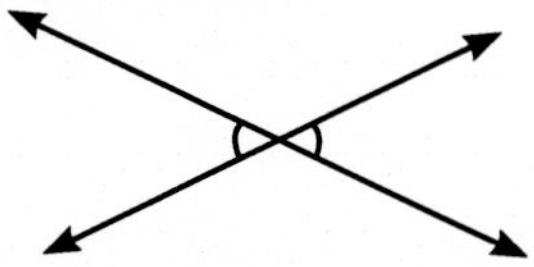

Ángulos Verticales — Ángulos no adyacentes con un vértice en común formado por dos rectas intersecantes.

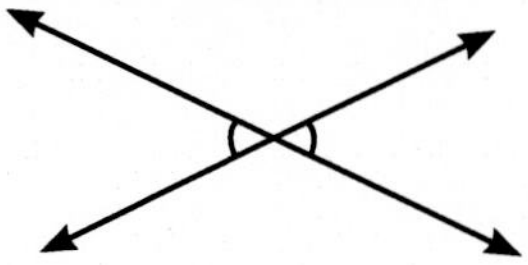

| Volume | The number of cubic units needed to fill a solid. | Volumen | La cantidad de unidades cúbicas necesitadas para llenar un sólido. |

x-axis — The horizontal number line on a coordinate plane.

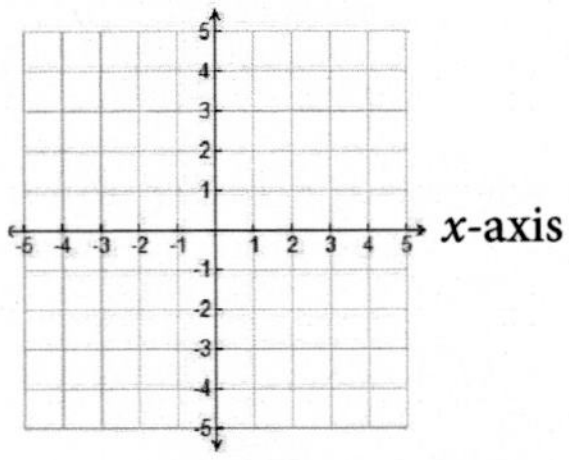

x-axis

Eje-x, Eje de la x — La recta numérica horizontal en un plano de coordenadas.

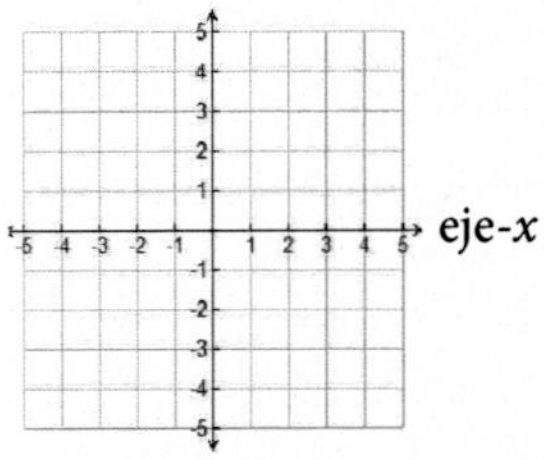

eje-x

y-axis	The vertical number line on a coordinate plane.	Eje-*y*, Eje de la *y*	La recta numérica vertical en un plano de coordenadas.

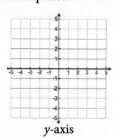

y-axis

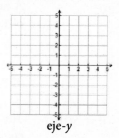

eje-*y*

y-Intercept	The point where a graph intersects the *y*-axis.	Intersección *y*	El punto donde una gráfica interseca el eje-*y*.

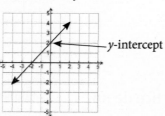

y-intercept

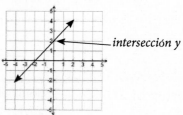

intersección y

Zero Pair	One positive integer chip paired with one negative integer chip.	Par Cero	Un chip entero positivo emparejado con un chip entero negativo.

● + ● = 0

1 + (−1) = 0

● + ● = 0

1 + (−1) = 0

SELECTED ANSWERS

BLOCK 1

Lesson 1

1. 1, 2, 4 composite **3.** 1, 2, 4, 8 composite **5.** 1, 2, 7, 14 composite 7. 1, 29 prime **9.** 1, 3, 9, 27 composite
11. 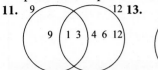 **13.**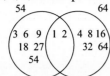

15. 9: 1,③ 9 **17.** 48: 1, 2, 3, 4, 6, 8,12, ⑯ 24, 48
   6: 1, 2,③ 6   32: 1, 2, 4, 8, ⑯ 32
                   64: 1, 2, 4, 8, ⑯ 32, 64
19. 24: 1,② 3, 4, 6, 8, 12, 24
   40: 1,② 4, 5, 8, 10, 20, 40
   54: 1,② 3, 6, 9, 18, 27, 54
21. Prime factor trees may vary: $18 = 3 \times 3 \times 2$
   $24 = 3 \times 2 \times 2 \times 2$ GCF $= 3 \times 2 = 6$
23. Prime factor trees may vary: $84 = 2 \times 2 \times 3 \times 7$
   $56 = 2 \times 2 \times 2 \times 7$ GCF $= 2 \times 2 \times 7 = 28$
25. 18 candy bars

Lesson 2

1. a) b) c) $\frac{1}{3}$ ▮▭▭ $\frac{2}{6}$ ▦▭▭▭▭▭ **d)** yes $\frac{1}{3}$ is the
same as $\frac{2}{6}$ **3.** $\frac{2}{5}$ ▦▦▭▭▭ , $\frac{5}{6}$ ▦▦▦▦▦▭ **5.** No,
they are not equivalent. The model for $\frac{5}{8}$ has less colored in
than the model for $\frac{3}{4}$. **7.** 4 **9.** 30 **11.** 3 **13.** 6 **15.** 4 **17.** 9 **19.**
Answers may vary $\frac{2}{6}, \frac{3}{9}$ **21.** Answers may vary $\frac{2}{5}, \frac{8}{20}$ **23.**
Answers may vary $\frac{12}{18}$ **25.** Yes. $\frac{3}{9}$ is equivalent to $\frac{1}{3}$ **27.** 1, 11
prime **29.** 1, 3, 13, 39 composite **31.** 4

Lesson 3

1. simplest form **3.** $\frac{4}{5}$ **5.** simplest form **7.** $\frac{1}{3}$ **9.** simplest
form **11.** $\frac{2}{7}$ **13.** $\frac{3}{5}$ **15.** $\frac{1}{3}$ **17.** $\frac{3}{8}$ **19.** $\frac{2}{5}$ **21.** $\frac{8}{9}$ **23.** $\frac{12}{24} = \frac{1}{2}$
and $\frac{16}{36} = \frac{4}{9}$ - no they are not equivalent **25.** answers may
vary **27.** $\frac{3}{8}$ **29.** $\frac{36}{126} = \frac{2}{7}$ of the students **31.** answers may
vary $\frac{2}{6}$ **33.** answers may vary $\frac{4}{5}$ **35.** 2

Lesson 4

1. 2, 4, 6, 8, 10 **3.** 14, 28, 42, 56, 70 **5.** 20 **7.** 30 **9.** 24 **11.** 70
13. 42 **15.** 60 **17.** 35 **19.** 14 **21.** 24 **23.** Friday **25.** Tuesday
27. 15 **29.** 6 **31.** 30 **33.** 5

Lesson 5

1. $\frac{2}{3}$ $\frac{4}{5}$ **3.** < **5.** = **7.** > **9.** < **11.** > **13.** $\frac{1}{5}, \frac{1}{3}, \frac{2}{5}$ **15.** $\frac{3}{10}, \frac{2}{5}, \frac{7}{10}$,
17. $\frac{3}{10}, \frac{2}{5}, \frac{7}{10}$ **19.** Answers may vary $\frac{7}{15}$ **21.** Answers may
vary $\frac{1}{3}$ **23.** Answers may vary $\frac{1}{2}$ **25.** Worker bees **27.** Yellow
29. 60 **31.** 28 **33.** 12 **35.** $\frac{1}{10}$ **37.** simplest form

Lesson 6

1. $\frac{7}{5}$ and $1\frac{2}{5}$ **3.** $\frac{7}{2}$ and $3\frac{1}{2}$ **5.** $\frac{11}{6}$ **7.** $\frac{18}{5}$ **9.** $\frac{43}{10}$ **11.** $\frac{17}{2}$
13. $\frac{361}{12}$ feet **15.** $2\frac{1}{3}$ **17.** $3\frac{1}{3}$ **19.** $4\frac{4}{7}$ **21.** $3\frac{1}{3}$ **23.** $6\frac{18}{25}$ feet
25. $3\frac{1}{4}, \frac{7}{2}, \frac{9}{2}$ **27.** $1\frac{1}{8}, \frac{3}{2}, \frac{7}{4}$ **29.** $10\frac{5}{8}$ inches **31.** 15 **33.** 40
35. > **37.** 18 **39.** 5

Lesson 7

1. 16 **3.** 3 in **5.** 10 in **7.** 11 in **9.** $4\frac{1}{4}$ in **11.** $6\frac{1}{4}$ in **13.** $3\frac{1}{4}$ in
15. $4\frac{3}{4}$ in **17.** draw line $\frac{3}{8}$ in **19.** draw line $2\frac{1}{2}$ in **21.** draw
line 4 inches **23.** $\frac{1}{2}$ in **25.** red and green **27.** the yellow
piece of yarn **29.** $\frac{3}{16}, \frac{7}{16}, \frac{1}{2}$ **31.** $\frac{11}{18}, \frac{20}{27}, \frac{7}{9}$ **33.** $3\frac{1}{5}$

Block 1 Review

1. 1, 5 prime **3.** 1, 3, 7, 21 composite **5.** 7 **7.** 9 **9.** 8 **11.** Not
equivalent ▮▮▮▭▮▮▮▮▭▭▭▭▭ **13.** 8 **15.** 49
17. 9 **19.** Answers may vary $\frac{3}{5}$ and $\frac{12}{20}$ **21.** $\frac{3}{4}$ **23.** $\frac{4}{5}$ **25.**
$\frac{8}{27}$ **27.** $\frac{11}{100}$ of a ton **29.** $\frac{2}{5}$ and $\frac{12}{25}$ - Not Equivalent **31.** 15,
30, 45, 60, 75 **33.** 40 **35.** 96 **37.** 24 **39.** 30 days **41.** > **43.**
$\frac{3}{10}, \frac{2}{5}, \frac{3}{5}$ **45.** $\frac{2}{5}, \frac{3}{7}, \frac{4}{5}$ **47.** Monday **49.** $\frac{29}{11}$ **51.** $3\frac{1}{2}$ **53.** $3\frac{1}{11}$
55. $1\frac{1}{3}, \frac{5}{3}, \frac{11}{6}$ **57.** $5\frac{1}{2}$ **59.** 4 in **61.** $3\frac{1}{2}$ in **63.** draw line $5\frac{1}{8}$
in **65.** draw line $\frac{7}{16}$ in

BLOCK 2

Lesson 8

1. $\frac{1}{2}$ **3.** 0 **5.** 2 **7.** 1 **9.** $\frac{1}{2}$ **11.** about $\frac{1}{2}$ of a pie **13.** 8 **15.** 16 **17.**
25 **19.** 3 **21.** 5 **23.** about 41 miles **25.** approx. 14 feet **27.** $\frac{11}{3}$
29. 5, 10, 15, 20, 25 **31.** 8, 16, 24, 32, 40

Lesson 9

1. $\frac{1}{2}$ **3.** $\frac{3}{4}$ **5.** $1\frac{1}{3}$ **7.** $\frac{1}{4}$ **9.** $\frac{6}{11}$ **11.** $\frac{1}{5}$ mile **13.** $1\frac{1}{2}$ **15.** $\frac{5}{6}$ **17.**
$\frac{1}{6}$ **19.** $\frac{2}{9}$ **21.** $\frac{1}{12}$ meter **23.** $\frac{3}{4}$ of her students **25.** draw line
$2\frac{1}{8}$ in **27.** draw line $1\frac{1}{2}$ in **29.** 1

Lesson 10

1. 9 **3.** $3\frac{3}{4}$ **5.** $5\frac{7}{10}$ **7.** $5\frac{11}{12}$ **9.** $4\frac{7}{12}$ **11.** $5\frac{1}{3}$ inches **13.** $1\frac{1}{2}$
15. $3\frac{1}{2}$ **17.** $1\frac{11}{15}$ **19.** $2\frac{19}{30}$ **21.** $\frac{2}{3}$ **23.** $\frac{3}{4}$ hour **25.** $3\frac{1}{5}$ more
tons **27.** $\frac{19}{20}$ **29.** $\frac{3}{10}$ **31.** $\frac{43}{60}$

Lesson 11

1. Answers may vary **3.** $7\frac{2}{5}$ **5.** $8\frac{1}{2}$ **7.** $12\frac{1}{4}$ **9.** $1\frac{7}{10}$ **11.** $\frac{5}{6}$
13. $3\frac{3}{8}$ **15.** $4\frac{1}{2}$ inches **17.** $5\frac{3}{10}$ miles **19.** $1\frac{2}{3}$ minutes **21.**
$1\frac{3}{8}$ feet **23.** Answers may vary **25.** $\frac{1}{9}$ **27.** $\frac{7}{12}$ **29.** $\frac{11}{24}$

Lesson 12

1. $1\frac{1}{2}$ inches **3.** 6 inches **5.** $6\frac{1}{4}$ inches **7.** Answers may vary
9. $2\frac{3}{4}$ inches **11.** 5 inches **13.** 7 inches **15.** $6\frac{7}{8}$ inches **17.**
$6\frac{1}{2}$ inches **19.** $111\frac{3}{4}$ yards **21.** $5\frac{1}{3}$ **23.** $6\frac{1}{12}$ **25.** $10\frac{19}{24}$ **27.**
$9\frac{1}{3}$

Block 2 Review

1. $\frac{1}{2}$ **3.** $\frac{1}{2}$ **5.** 1 **7.** 4 **9.** 2 **11.** 14 **13.** $\frac{5}{8}$ **15.** $\frac{2}{3}$ **17.** $1\frac{8}{15}$ **19.** $\frac{23}{45}$
21. $\frac{31}{36}$ **23.** $\frac{5}{24}$ **25.** $4\frac{1}{4}$ **27.** $3\frac{1}{4}$ **29.** $7\frac{11}{21}$ **31.** $1\frac{17}{18}$ **33.** $6\frac{1}{2}$
35. $1\frac{5}{7}$ **37.** $3\frac{9}{10}$ **39.** $1\frac{2}{3}$ **41.** $5\frac{7}{8}$ **43.** 11 inches **45.** $12\frac{5}{8}$
47. $2\frac{3}{4}$ **49.** $281\frac{1}{2}$ feet

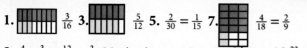

BLOCK 3

Lesson 13

1. $\frac{3}{16}$ **3.** $\frac{5}{12}$ **5.** $\frac{2}{30} = \frac{1}{15}$ **7.** $\frac{4}{18} = \frac{2}{9}$
9. $\frac{4}{5} \times \frac{3}{4} = \frac{12}{20} = \frac{3}{5}$ **11.** $\frac{1}{6}$ of a cup **13.** 2 **15.** $1\frac{1}{2}$ **17.** $10\frac{23}{28}$

Lesson 14

1. $\frac{4}{15}$ **3.** $\frac{2}{15}$ **5.** $\frac{1}{7}$ **7.** $\frac{6}{35}$ **9.** $\frac{7}{12}$ **11.** $\frac{1}{4}$ of the routine **13.** $\frac{2}{5}$
15. $\frac{3}{14}$ **17.** $\frac{9}{13}$ **19.** $\frac{5}{12}$ **21.** $\frac{1}{2}$ of the shots **23.** $\frac{5}{8}$ hour **25.** 10
27. 6 inches **29.** 29 inches

Lesson 15

1. a) $\frac{3}{4} \div \frac{1}{4}$ **b) c)** **d)** 3 **3.** 2
5. 3 **7.** 2 **9.** $\frac{4}{5} \div \frac{2}{5} = 2$
11. $\frac{6}{12} \div \frac{2}{12} = 3$ OR $\frac{1}{2} \div \frac{2}{12} = 3$ OR $\frac{6}{12} \div \frac{1}{6} = 3$ OR
$\frac{1}{2} \div \frac{1}{6} = 3$ **13.** $\frac{6}{8} \div \frac{2}{8} = 3$ OR $\frac{3}{4} \div \frac{2}{8} = 3$ OR $\frac{6}{8} \div \frac{1}{4} = 3$ OR
$\frac{3}{4} \div \frac{1}{4} = 3$ **15.** 4 times **17.** 8 sections **19.** $\frac{3}{8}$ **21.** 20 **23.** 30
25. $1\frac{19}{24}$

Lesson 16

1. 2 **3.** 4 **5.** 6 **7.** 4 **9.** 3 **11. a)** 2 **b)** 2 **c)** 4 **d)** 6 **13.** $1\frac{3}{7}$ **15.**
$1\frac{2}{3}$ **17.** $1\frac{3}{7}$ **19.** $1\frac{1}{2}$ **21.** $5\frac{1}{3}$ sections **23.** $\frac{6}{8} \div \frac{2}{8} = 3$ OR
$\frac{3}{4} \div \frac{2}{8} = 3$ OR $\frac{6}{8} \div \frac{1}{4} = 3$ OR $\frac{3}{4} \div \frac{1}{4} = 3$ **25.** $\frac{7}{8}$ **27.** $5\frac{11}{15}$

Lesson 17

1. a) answers may vary **b)** answers may vary **3.** 11 or 12 **5.**
12 **7.** 6 **9.** about 15 fly balls **11.** 18 **13.** 28 **15.** 14 **17.** 2 **19.** 9
21. 6 **23.** Approx. 7 days **25.** About 30 cups **27.** $\frac{3}{8}$ **29.** $\frac{7}{20}$
31. 2

Lesson 18

1. 4 **3.** 15 **5.** $5\frac{1}{3}$ **7.** 10 medals **9.** $19\frac{1}{5}$ windows **11.** 10 **13.**
15 **15.** 12 **17.** 15 people **19.** $22\frac{1}{2}$ trips **21.** $5\frac{1}{2}$ inches **23.** 5
inches **25.** 6 **27.** 5 **29.** 10

Lesson 19

1. $4\frac{1}{4}$ **3.** 11 **5.** $1\frac{1}{8}$ **7.** 4 **9.** $9\frac{1}{6}$ **11.** $7\frac{7}{8}$ cups of flour **13.** 4
15. $9\frac{1}{3}$ **17.** $5\frac{5}{9}$ **19.** $2\frac{4}{5}$ **21.** 7 paving stones **23.** $\frac{3}{10}$ **25.** $\frac{1}{14}$
27. $4\frac{2}{3}$ **29.** $10\frac{2}{3}$ **31.** $16\frac{1}{2}$

Lesson 20

1. 10 units² **3.** $8\frac{7}{16}$ units² **5.** $\frac{11}{32}$ inches² **7.** $381\frac{1}{4}$ feet² **9.**
$5\frac{4}{9}$ units² **11.** $14\frac{1}{16}$ inches² **13.** $8\frac{17}{64}$ **15.** $1\frac{17}{64}$ **17.** $\frac{1}{4}$ inch²
19. $\frac{117}{128}$ inches² **21.** $3\frac{11}{64}$ **23.** Answers may vary **25.** $2\frac{7}{9}$ **27.**
11 **29.** $1\frac{17}{21}$

Block 3 Review

1. $\frac{1}{2} \times \frac{3}{4} = \frac{3}{8}$ **3.** $\frac{3}{5} \times \frac{3}{4} = \frac{9}{20}$ **5.** **7.** $\frac{2}{10} = \frac{1}{5}$ **7.** $\frac{1}{4}$ **9.** $\frac{5}{9}$
11. $\frac{3}{10}$ **13.** $\frac{1}{8}$ of the cars **15.** $\frac{1}{12}$ of the basket of chicken
17. $\frac{3}{4} \div \frac{1}{4} = 3$ **19.** 3 **21.** 4 **23.** 4 **25.** $\frac{6}{7}$
27. $\frac{9}{10}$ **29.** 4 times **31.** 10 or 11 **33.** 2 **35.** 9 **37.** 9 laps **39.** 8
41. 12 **43.** $25\frac{1}{2}$ **45.** 40 **47.** 30 **49.** $3\frac{5}{12}$ **51.** $1\frac{11}{24}$ **53.** $5\frac{20}{21}$
55. $6\frac{8}{13}$ **57.** $10\frac{1}{2}$ inches² **59.** $6\frac{3}{4}$ inches² **61.** $27\frac{1}{8}$ units²
63. $3\frac{1}{16}$ inches² **65.** $2\frac{1}{4}$ inches²

BLOCK 4

Lesson 21

1. 1.12 **3.** 2.39 **5.** 0.3 **7.** 2.3 **9. a)** thousandths **b)** ones **c)**
tenths **d)** hundredths **11.** eight thousandths **13.** three cones
15. 99.2 **17.** 52.06 **19.** 0.223 **21.** thirty-five and eighty-seven
hundredths **23.** five hundred forty-nine thousandths **25.**
sixty-eight and four tenths **27.** $\frac{3}{8}$ **29.** $1\frac{2}{5}$ **31.** $\frac{11}{12}$ **33.** 8

Lesson 22

1. 4 **3.** 7 **5.** 18 **7.** approx. 2 hours **9.** 34. 9 **11.** 71.3 **13.**
3.9 **15.** $2.40 **17.** 45.21 **19.** 321.24 **21.** 3.90 **23.** 7.909 **25.**
201.109 **27.** 5.001 **29.** 1.34 **31.** 0.27 **33.** seventy and seven
hundredths **35.** $5\frac{1}{16}$ inches² **37.** $3\frac{7}{16}$ inches²

Lesson 23

1. < **3.** > **5.** > **7.** > **9.** < **11.** 17.8, 17.801, 17.81, 17.851 **13.** C.
6.9 **15.** D. 8.8 **17.** 51.5 and 50.98 seconds **19.** 48.9 and 49.09
seconds **21.** 49.76 seconds **23.** Friday **25.** Washington **27.**
Idaho, Nevada, Alaska, California, Oregon, Washington **29.**
32.63 **31.** 2.17 **33.** 6.4

Lesson 24

1. 8 **3.** 13 **5.** 7 **7.** 26 **9.** 22 **11.** About $15.00 **13.** 16 **15.** 27
17. 216 **19.** About $209.00 **21.** 5 **23.** 3 **25.** 1 **27.** approx. 10
books **29.** = **31.** 32.34, 32.4, 32.43, 32.48 **33.** 11.02, 11.022,
11.2, 11.22 **35.** $1\frac{1}{2}$ **37.** $4\frac{1}{10}$ **39.** $26\frac{1}{3}$

Lesson 25

1. 5.5 **3.** 13.206 **5.** 7.105 **7.** $20.13 **9.** 2.56 **11.** 2.86 **13.** 3.649
15. 8.31 inches **17.** 9.36 more inches **19.** 14.09 inches **21.**
10.92 inches **23.** $204.37 **25.** Answers may vary **27.** 4.68 **29.**
4.381 **31.** $7\frac{1}{2}$ **33.** $5\frac{7}{15}$ **35.** $1\frac{3}{5}$

Lesson 26

1. 12.3 **3.** $15.19 **5.** $24.45 **7.** $5.85 **9.** 23.68 **11.** 34.44 **13.**
19.448 **15.** 0.45 **17.** $0.28 **19.** $2.76 **21.** 0.0525 **23.** $\frac{5}{12}, \frac{1}{2}, \frac{2}{3}$
25. 1.089, 1.31, 1.4 **27.** $\frac{3}{10}, \frac{7}{20}, \frac{2}{5}$ **29.** $10\frac{1}{8}$ inches² **31.** $10\frac{9}{16}$
inches²

Lesson 27

1. 1.9 **3.** 7.3 **5.** 2.8 **7.** $1.49 **9.** $0.12 **11.** 0.0875 **13.** 0.098 **15.**
1.15 **17.** $1.50 **19.** 1.24 **21.** 3.97 **23.** 5.37 **25. a)** 9 **b)** 8 **27. a)**
8 **b)** 11

Lesson 28

1. 48 ÷ 8 **3.** 1240 ÷ 34 **5.** 182.9 ÷ 31 **7.** 9 **9.** 70 **11.** 35 **13.** 65.6 **15.** $\frac{1}{7}$ **17.** 3.45 times greater **19.** 4.4 **21.** 4 **23.** 10 **25.** $1.28/pound **27.** 1.6 times greater **29.** 42.84 **31.** 0.20 **33.** 7.25

Lesson 29

1. 10 **3.** 5 *cm* **5.** 14.1 *cm* **7.** 9 *cm* **9.** 14.1 *cm* **11.** 4.1 *cm* **13. a)** answers may vary **b)** 6.6 *cm* **c)** Answers may vary **15.** 7.5 *cm* **17.** 16.5 *cm* **19. a)** answers may vary **b)** 7.5 *cm* **c)** Answers may vary **21.** draw line 3.4 *cm* **23.** draw line 5.7 *cm* **25.** draw line 0.9 **27.** 15.2 *cm* **29.** 20.58 **31.** 14.2 **33.** 156

Lesson 30

1. P = 13.8 *cm* A = 7.7 *cm²* **3.** P = 14.4 *m²* A = 7.475 *mm²* **5.** P = 17.6 *mm* A = 14.95 *mm²* **7. a)** 12.8 *cm* **b)** 18.49 *cm²* **9.** 6.8 *cm* **11.** 10.5 *cm* **13. a)** 95.2 *m* **b)** 566.44 *m²* **15.** 4.2 *cm²* **17.** 1.89 *cm²* **19.** $3\frac{1}{2}$ **21.** $\frac{1}{3}$ **23.** $5\frac{1}{4}$ **25.** 12 **27.** 9 pounds

Block 4 Review

1. 1.34 **3.** 0.28 **5.** tenths **7.** 2.7 **9.** 0.28 **11.** nine and fifteen hundredths **13.** 52.99 **15.** 6.359 **17.** 9.0 **19.** 93.01 **21.** 60 **23.** $1.40 **25.** < **27.** = **29.** > **31.** 0.8, 0.842, 0.88, 0.884 **33.** 13. **35.** 28 **37.** 29 **39.** Approx. 13 pounds **41.** 9 **43.** About 29 miles **45.** 1.299 **47.** 16.048 **49.** 13.064 **51.** 1.96 **53.** 8.15 ounces **55.** 29.2 **57.** 55.25 **59.** 29.281 **61.** 0.24 **63.** 9.4472 **65.** $59.97 **67.** 4.51 **69.** 0.3 **71.** 0.06 **73.** 9.09 **75.** 0.14 pounds **77.** 4.39 **79.** 87.07 **81.** 5.15 **83.** 28 servings **85.** 9.3 *cm* **87.** 1.7 *cm* **89.** 2 *cm* **91. a)** Answers may vary **b)** 7.9 *cm* **c)** Answers may vary **93.** draw line 7.2 *cm* **95.** P = 14.6 *cm* A = 13.12 *cm²* **97.** P = 19.7 *mm* A = 17.755 *mm²* **99.** P = 9.4 *cm* A = 5.4 *cm²*

INDEX

of fractions, 77
of mixed numbers

R
Reciprocals, 81

Rectangle
  area of, 97
  area formula, 97
  perimeter, 60

Rounding
  decimals, 114
  fractions, 42
  mixed numbers, 42

S
Simplest form, 13
  common factors, 13
  greatest common factor, 14
Square
  area of, 98
  area formula, 98

Subtraction
  of decimals, 124
  of fractions, 47
  of mixed numbers, 51

T
Tick marks, 30

Triangle
  area of, 98
    Explore! Triangle Area, 98
  area formula, 98
  base of, 98
  height of, 98
  vertex of, 98

U
Units, see customary system and metric
system

V
Venn diagram, 3

W
Whole numbers, 89
  as fractions, 89
  multiplying by fractions, 89
  dividing decimals by, 133
  dividing by fractions, 89

X Y Z

PROBLEM - SOLVING

UNDERSTAND THE SITUATION

- ► Read then re-read the problem.
- ► Identify what the problem is asking you to find.
- ► Locate the key information.

PLAN YOUR APPROACH

Choose a strategy to solve the problem:

- ► Guess, check and revise
- ► Use an equation
- ► Use a formula
- ► Draw a picture
- ► Draw a graph
- ► Make a table
- ► Make a chart
- ► Make a list
- ► Look for patterns
- ► Compute or simplify

STOP AND THINK

- ► Did you answer the question that was asked?
- ► Does your answer make sense?
- ► Does your answer have the correct units?
- ► Look back over your work and correct any mistakes.

SOLVE THE PROBLEM

- ► Use your strategy to solve the problem.
- ► Show all work.

DEFEND YOUR ANSWER

Show that your answer is correct by doing one of the following:

- ► Use a second strategy to get the same answer.
- ► Verify that your first calculations are accurate by repeating your process.

ANSWER THE QUESTION

- ► State your answer in a complete sentence.
- ► Include the appropriate units.

MATHEMATICS PROBLEM-SOLVING SCORING GUIDE

Reprinted with permission from the Oregon Department of Education.

	CONCEPTUAL UNDERSTANDING *Interpreting the concepts of the task and translating them into mathematics.*	PROCESSES AND STRATEGIES *Choosing strategies that can work, and then carrying out the strategies chosen.*	VERIFICATION *In addition to solving the task, <u>identifiable evidence</u> of a second look at the concepts/strategies/ calculations to defend a solution.*	COMMUNICATION *Using pictures, symbols, and/or vocabulary to convey the path toward the identified solution.*
	WHAT?	**HOW?**	**DEFEND!**	**THE CONNECTION PATH!**
6	The task is changed into thoroughly developed ideas **and** is enhanced by other math ideas.	Complex and/or enhanced processes and strategies are used to sole the task.	The second time solving the task is enhanced, possibly by solving with a new strategy.	The path connecting concepts and strategies to the identified answer is very clear and enhanced possibly by graphics or examples.
5	The task is changed into thoroughly developed math ideas that work.	A thoroughly developed plan using pictures, charts, words, graphs, and/or symbols solves the task.	The second time solving the task is clear, and thoroughly develoed, checking all parts of the work.	The path through all parts of the work toward the identified answer is thoroughly developed.
4	The task is changed into complete math ideas that can work.	A complete plan using pictures, charts, words, graphs, and/or symbols is used to solve the task (all work is shown).	The check completely solves the task a second time checking ideas, math steps, **and** a solution.	The path through the work toward the identified answer is complete.
3	Parts of the task are changed into math ideas that work.	The plan could solve parts of the task **or** the work is only partly shown.	Some parts but not all of the work is checked.	The path through the work is partly shown.
2	The concepts of the task are underdeveloped **or** the task is changed into some ideas that do not work.	The plan is underdeveloped (many missing sections) **or** the plan includes some strategies that cannot work.	The check is underdeveloped (only a small section of the work is checked).	The path is not clear or is underdeveloped showing few connectins within the work.
1	Inappropriate **or** minimal concepts are used **or** no ideas are shown.	The plan is ineffective, the work is minimal, the work conflicts with the answer given **or** no work is shown.	The check is ineffective for the task, is only minimal, **or** no identifiable check is shown.	The path is ineffective, minimal, **or** is not shown at all.

ACCURACY:

5) The answer is correct **and** the work supports it.	**4)** The work had a small mistake but the important parts of the work are fine.	**1)** The answer is not correct, not finished, or does not match the work.